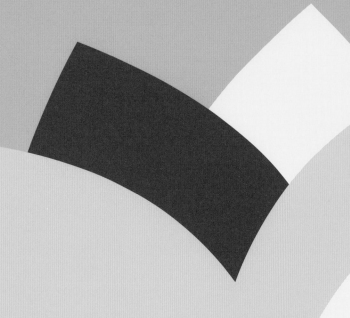

Eat plants, be happy!

Eat plants, be happy!

VICKI VALSAMIS · CAROLINE GRIFFITHS

Smith Street Books

Contents

Eat Plants, Be Happy! ... 6

Flowers, Shoots & Stems ... 10

Leaves & Leafy Greens ... 36

Seeds & Pods ... 62

Fruiting Veg ... 88

Squash ... 114

Brassicas ... 140

Roots ... 168

Tubers ... 194

Bulbs & Fungi ... 220

Index ... 246

To the memory of my wonderful mother, Doreen.
And, to the future with my boys Kaine, Iefan and Bryn. – **CG**

·

To my beautiful parents Margaret and Peter for always instilling the importance
of love and joy in the kitchen. This book is very much for you. – **VV**

We all want to be happy, right? Surely, one of the simplest paths to happiness is through our happy bellies. How to make happy bellies? Eat plants!

Let's focus on veg as the foundation and building blocks of boldly flavourful meals. Eating an abundance of plants not only nourishes our bodies, it can lift our spirits and soothe our souls.

We think everyone should eat more plants, and we don't just mean two carrots instead of one – it's about enjoying all the colours of the veggie rainbow. The nutritional benefits are clear and well documented, and broadening our horizons when it comes to the types of vegetables we eat will only increase those benefits – not to mention the greater variety of incredible food.

Veggies, in all their wonderful and sometimes weird forms, too often play second fiddle in a meal, and we're here to change that mindset. With a staggering array of tastes, textures and culinary opportunities, there's absolutely no reason why good-quality produce shouldn't be the star of its own show.

When shopping, though, be mindful. We love seasonal fare, and while it's convenient to be able to buy practically any vegetable at any time of year from a supermarket, if you're buying veg out of season, it means they're travelling long distances to get to those shelves. Fresh produce typically contains higher levels of nutrients at harvest, and the longer those veggies sit in transit, the fewer nutrients remain. Produce meant for long hauls is generally not allowed to fully ripen before harvest, resulting in vegetables that may taste bland and uninspiring – not to mention their carbon footprint.

Go to a farmers' market or your local greengrocer, instead, and have a chat to the person selling the produce. They'll be able to tell you what's good. Buying in season can be lighter on your wallet too, as anything that's in abundance will be cheaper.

Your body will also thank you – more and more studies are showing the links between mood and food. Our feelings of general well-being; the health of our gut; and mental, brain and physical health are all connected with our diet – of which plant foods like vegetables, fruits, legumes (such as chickpeas, lentils and tofu), wholegrains and raw nuts should be the main ingredients.

In this book, we share our collection of recipes intended to make plants the hero. There are large and small dishes that can be easily paired to make up a larger meal, and all of the recipes include a note on the time of year the produce is in season. There are heaps of tips and helpful substitutions to veganise recipes – all highlighted with icons on the pages. Vegetarians, vegans and flexitarians alike will find this book packed with approachable, delicious, veggie-packed recipes.

Happy cooking!

Flowers, Shoots & Stems

artichoke

asparagus

banana blossom

bok choy

celery

choy sum

fennel

pea shoots

rhubarb

zucchini flowers

Ricotta-stuffed zucchini flowers

MAKES 20

The delicate and beautiful zucchini flower was once discarded by many ... can you imagine? This is a real stand-alone dish, no accompaniments required – just a glass of wine and an appetite. –VV

150 g (5½ oz/1 cup) cornflour (corn starch)

75 g (2¾ oz/½ cup) self-raising flour, plus extra for dusting

375 ml (1½ cups) iced water

140 g (5 oz/heaped ½ cup) fresh ricotta

1 tablespoon finely grated lemon zest

3 tablespoons chopped basil

3 tablespoons chopped dill

50 g (1¾ oz/½ cup) finely grated pecorino

½ teaspoon freshly ground black pepper

½ teaspoon sea salt

20 baby zucchini (courgettes), with flowers attached

vegetable oil, for deep-frying

Place the cornflour, flour and iced water in a bowl, mixing with a spoon until just combined but still a bit lumpy. Allow to stand for 15 minutes.

In another bowl, place the ricotta, lemon zest, basil, dill, pecorino, pepper and salt. Mix together with a spoon.

Using a teaspoon, gently spoon the ricotta mixture into each zucchini flower, then twist the petals around to enclose the filling.

Fill a deep, medium-sized saucepan with 5–6 cm (2–2½ in) vegetable oil. Place over high heat until hot.

Meanwhile, spread some extra flour on a flat plate. Dust each zucchini with the flour, setting them aside on a tray until the oil is heated through.

One by one, dip each floured zucchini into the batter, then carefully lower into the hot oil and cook in small batches, four or five at a time, for 2 minutes, or until the batter is golden. Remove with a slotted spoon and drain on paper towel.

Transfer to a serving platter and serve hot.

BEST IN: SPRING & SUMMER

MAKE IT VEGAN!
Use vegan pecorino (or parmesan) and substitute the ricotta for silken tofu. Press out any liquid and blend or mash the tofu to the consistency of ricotta.

Fresh artichoke salad with lemon, celery & herbs

SERVES 4

This is a light, refreshing salad with a fabulous crunch, courtesy of the wheat grains, which you will find in delicatessens and health-food stores. If you have an aversion to wheat, quinoa works well too. –VV

1 tablespoon extra virgin olive oil

55 g (2 oz/¼ cup) wheat grains

1 lemon

10 large globe artichokes

140 g (5 oz) celery, finely sliced on the diagonal

3 tablespoons chopped parsley

2 tablespoons chopped mint

small handful of snow pea (mangetout) shoots

75 g (2¾ oz/¾ cup) shaved parmesan

LEMON YOGHURT DRESSING

90 g (3 oz/⅓ cup) Greek-style yoghurt

½ teaspoon grated lemon zest

½ teaspoon sea salt

½ teaspoon freshly ground black pepper

LEMON VINAIGRETTE

60 ml (¼ cup) lemon juice

60 ml (¼ cup) extra virgin olive oil

MAKE IT VEGAN!
Omit the parmesan (or use a vegan option) and use dairy-free yoghurt.

In a small bowl, whisk together the lemon yoghurt dressing ingredients until smooth. Cover and set aside in the fridge.

Warm the olive oil in a small frying pan over medium heat. Add the wheat grains, and, stirring constantly, cook for 2–3 minutes, or until light brown. Transfer to a plate to cool.

Cut the lemon in half and squeeze the juice into a large bowl. Add the lemon halves to the bowl and fill halfway with cold water.

Using a serrated knife, trim the artichoke stems, leaving 5 cm (2 in) of stem attached. Working with one artichoke at a time, trim off the outer leaves by pulling them back and breaking them off to expose the tender green heart. Cut one-third off the top, then use a vegetable peeler to clean the base and stem of the artichoke. Place immediately in the bowl of lemon water while preparing the remaining artichokes, so they don't discolour.

In a small bowl, whisk together the lemon vinaigrette ingredients. Season with salt and freshly ground black pepper.

Drain the artichokes in a colander, then finely slice, using a sharp knife or mandoline.

Transfer to a large mixing bowl and drizzle with the lemon vinaigrette. Add the celery, parsley, mint and pea shoots, drizzle with the lemon yoghurt dressing and gently mix.

Transfer to a serving platter, top with the shaved parmesan and serve.

BEST IN: SPRING

Braised celery with blue cheese

SERVES 4

Most of us tend to think of celery as a salad vegetable – or as a vehicle for peanut butter – but it is also wonderful cooked as the hero of a dish. With gentle braising it becomes soft and tender, dressed here with a delicious glaze. –CG

10 celery stalks, trimmed, leaves reserved

30 g (1 oz) butter

2 shallots, finely sliced

2 garlic cloves, finely sliced

1 carrot, finely sliced

250 ml (1 cup) Vegetable stock (see page 23)

1 fresh oregano sprig

60 g (2 oz) creamy blue cheese, crumbled

MAKE IT VEGAN!
Replace the butter with olive oil and leave out the blue cheese (or use your favourite soft vegan cheese instead).

Remove the 'strings' from the celery, if necessary, by running a vegetable peeler over them. Cut the stalks on the diagonal into 3 cm (1¼ in) lengths.

Melt the butter in a large heavy-based frying pan with a lid over medium–high heat until foaming. Add the shallot and garlic and cook for 3–4 minutes, or until just starting to colour.

Add the carrot and cook for a further 2 minutes, then add the celery and continue to cook for 5 minutes, or until the celery is lightly browned at the edges. Season with salt and freshly ground black pepper, pour in the stock and add the oregano sprig. Cover and bring to the boil.

Reduce the heat to a simmer and cook, covered, for 15 minutes, or until the vegetables are almost tender. Remove the lid and increase the heat to medium–high. Simmer for about 5 minutes, or until the liquid is reduced slightly and glaze-like, and the vegetables are tender.

Serve the celery warm, with the juices poured over the top, scattered with the reserved celery leaves and the crumbled blue cheese.

BEST IN: LATE SUMMER & AUTUMN

Butter-poached asparagus with salt-cured egg yolks

SERVES 4

It's hard to beat the elegant simplicity of plump, perfectly poached asparagus spears. Here they are topped with an ethereal scattering of shaved umami-rich cured egg yolk. If you don't have time to cure the egg yolks (it is very simple to do, but does take four days), you can pair the poached asparagus with the miso hollandaise on page 147. For added effect, try using purple and white asparagus, when available. –CG

16 green, white or purple asparagus spears
(or any mix of the three)

20 g (¾ oz) butter

SALT-CURED EGG YOLKS

280 g (10 oz/1 cup) fine sea salt

1 teaspoon crushed chilli flakes

1 teaspoon freshly ground black pepper

1 bay leaf

55 g (2 oz/¼ cup) sugar

3 free-range egg yolks

MAKE IT VEGAN!
Replace the butter with olive oil and leave out the egg yolk. Drizzle with aquafaba mayo (see page 184), replacing the lemon juice with rice wine vinegar and adding 3 teaspoons of white miso paste.

For the salt-cured egg yolks, whiz the salt, chilli flakes, pepper and bay leaf in a food processor until the bay leaf is chopped. Stir in the sugar.

Spread half the seasoned salt mixture into a small dish, bowl or container. Using the back of a spoon, make three 'nests' in the mixture. Gently put an egg yolk in each nest, then carefully sprinkle the yolks with the remaining salt mixture. Cover with plastic wrap or a lid and refrigerate for 4 days.

Preheat the oven to 60°C/140°F (fan-forced). Remove the egg yolks from the salt mixture, brush off the excess with a clean pastry brush, and gently rinse the egg yolks under cold water. Place on a wire rack and bake for 2–3 hours, or until the yolks are firm enough to shave or grate.

Near serving time, trim the woody ends off the asparagus, if necessary, then peel the bottom third of the spears, if you like. Fill a large frying pan with water to a depth of about 2.5 cm (1 in) and bring to the boil. Add the butter to the frying pan with the asparagus and season generously with freshly ground black pepper. Simmer gently for 3–4 minutes, or until the asparagus is tender; the cooking time will depend on the thickness of the spears.

Transfer the asparagus to a serving plate and drizzle with some of the pan juices. Shave the egg yolks over the top, using a vegetable peeler or small knife. Serve immediately.

Any leftover egg yolk can be refrigerated in an airtight container for up to a week.

BEST IN: SPRING & SUMMER

Charred asparagus & broccolini with garlic olive crumbs

SERVES 4

Charring asparagus and broccolini under the grill is a simple and quick way to bring out their sweetness. Grilling asparagus works best with lovely thick spears, about the width of your finger. The golden crunchy crumbs add a wonderful textural contrast. –CG

3 thick slices ciabatta, about 100 g (3½ oz), most of the crusts removed

1½ tablespoons olive oil, plus extra for drizzling

45 g (1½ oz/¼ cup) pitted large green or kalamata olives, chopped

2 teaspoons chopped fresh thyme

1 garlic clove, crushed

finely grated zest of 1 lemon

175 g (6 oz) bunch of broccolini

16 asparagus spears

lemon wedges, to serve

ALREADY VEGAN!

Preheat the grill (broiler) to high. Line a baking tray with foil, folding up the edges of the foil to make a shallow border all the way round.

Tear the ciabatta into rough chunks and whiz in a food processor until coarsely chopped. Add the olive oil and whiz again.

Heat a large heavy-based frying pan over medium–high heat. Add the ciabatta crumbs, along with the olives, thyme and garlic. Cook, stirring occasionally, for 4–5 minutes, or until the breadcrumbs are golden and crisp. Stir in the lemon zest, remove from the heat and set aside.

Trim the ends off the broccolini, then cut any larger stalks in half lengthways. Trim the woody ends off the asparagus, then peel the bottom third of the spears, if you like. Place the vegetables on the baking tray and drizzle with olive oil. Toss to coat, then spread out in a single layer. Season lightly with salt and freshly ground black pepper.

Grill (broil) for 4–5 minutes, or until the vegetables are tender and well charred, turning after about 3 minutes. Remove any smaller stems if they cook more quickly.

Serve warm, sprinkled with the crumbs, with lemon wedges on the side.

BEST IN: SPRING & SUMMER

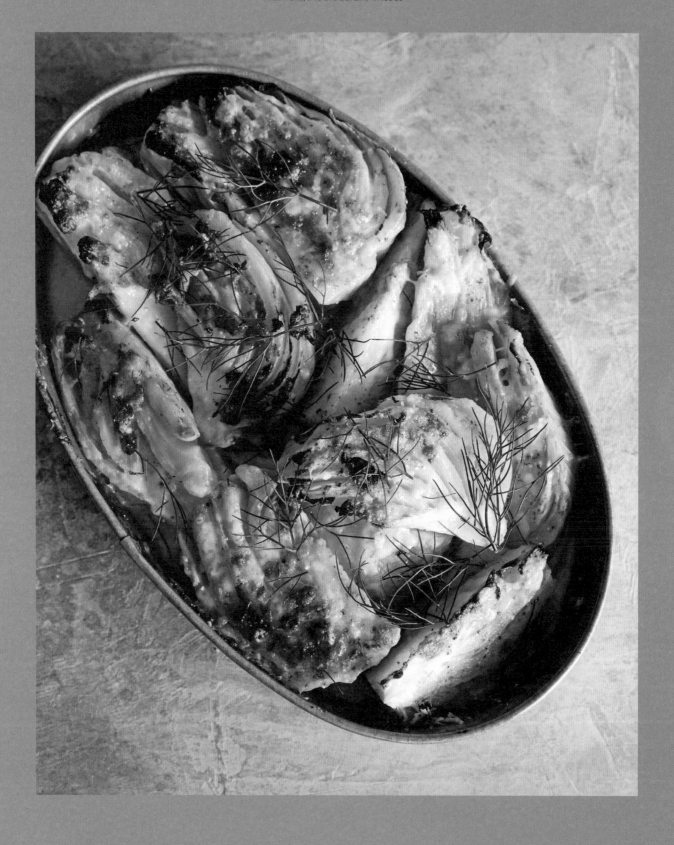

Fennel gratin

SERVES 4

Fennel is an extremely versatile vegetable and equally at home cooked or raw. The more mature bulbs are well suited to cooking, while the young tender bulbs are lovely finely shaved or sliced and used in delicate salads. Simple and honest, this is baked fennel at its finest. –CG

2 fennel bulbs, about 600 g (1 lb 5 oz) in total, with fronds

125 ml (½ cup) thickened (whipping) cream (35% fat)

nutmeg, for grating

25 g (1 oz/¼ cup) grated parmesan

Preheat the oven to 160°C/320°F (fan-forced). Grease a shallow baking dish, about 1.25 litres (5 cups) in capacity.

Trim the fennel stalks and bulbs, reserving a handful of the fronds for sprinkling over the baked gratin. Cut each bulb lengthways into six wedges, keeping the wedges attached at the base so they don't fall apart.

Bring a large saucepan of salted water to the boil. Add the fennel, return to the boil, then reduce the heat and simmer gently for 3 minutes, or until starting to soften. Drain well.

Arrange the fennel in the baking dish and season with salt and freshly ground black pepper. Drizzle the cream over, grate a little nutmeg on top and sprinkle with half the parmesan. Cover with foil and bake for 30 minutes.

Remove the dish from the oven and remove the foil. Sprinkle with the remaining parmesan and bake, uncovered, for a further 5–10 minutes, or until tender and lightly browned on top. If you need a little extra browning, finish the gratin under a hot grill (broiler) for a minute or two.

Serve warm, sprinkled with the reserved fennel fronds.

BEST IN: LATE SUMMER, AUTUMN & WINTER

Sumac chickpea salad with fennel & artichoke

SERVES 4–6

Sumac is a purplish berry widely used in Middle Eastern cuisines. Sold dried and ground, it adds a lovely tangy, lemony flavour when roasted with chickpeas, artichokes and fennel. This salad can also be served cold the next day, with a dollop of fresh yoghurt or hummus. –VV

1 lemon

4 globe artichokes

400 g (14 oz) tin chickpeas, rinsed and drained

1 teaspoon ground sumac

2 teaspoons pomegranate molasses

1 large fennel bulb

1 garlic clove, crushed

180 g (6½ oz/4 cups) baby rocket (arugula)

40 g (1½ oz/¼ cup) pitted kalamata olives, cut in half

GARLIC VINEGAR DRESSING

2½ tablespoons olive oil

1½ tablespoons red wine vinegar

1 tablespoon apple cider vinegar

1 garlic clove, crushed

½ teaspoon sea salt

Preheat the oven to 180°C/350°F (fan-forced). Line two baking trays with baking paper.

Cut the lemon in half and squeeze the juice into a large bowl. Add the lemon halves to the bowl and fill halfway with cold water.

Using a serrated knife, trim the artichoke stems, leaving 5 cm (2 in) of stem attached. Working with one artichoke at a time, trim off the outer leaves by pulling them back and breaking them off to expose the tender green heart. Cut one-third off the top, then use a vegetable peeler to clean the base and stem of the artichoke. Cut into quarters and immediately place in the bowl of lemon water while preparing the remaining artichokes, so they don't discolour.

Drain the artichokes well in a colander, then place in a mixing bowl. Add the chickpeas, sumac and pomegranate molasses and mix to coat thoroughly. Season with salt and freshly ground black pepper, then spread the mixture on one of the baking trays.

Cut the fennel in half lengthways. Trim the tops off, then cut the bulb into slices about 1 cm (½ in) thick. Spread the fennel on the other baking tray and season with salt and freshly ground black pepper.

Place both trays in the oven and bake for 25 minutes, turning the ingredients once. Remove from the oven and allow to cool completely.

In a bowl, whisk together the ingredients for the garlic vinegar dressing.

Transfer the cooled fennel and chickpea mixture to a mixing bowl. Add the garlic, rocket and olives and toss together gently.

Transfer to a serving platter, drizzle with the dressing and serve immediately.

ALREADY VEGAN!

BEST IN: LATE AUTUMN & SPRING

Fennel soup

SERVES 4

This soup is decadent and silky smooth, with rich aniseed notes. It's definitely worth making the vegetable stock from scratch, as it elevates the flavours, but if you are pressed for time, use a good-quality store-bought one. –VV

125 ml (½ cup) olive oil

4 large fennel bulbs, sliced, fronds reserved

3 leeks, white part only, sliced

4 teaspoons fennel seeds

1 potato, peeled and chopped

4 garlic cloves, chopped

sour cream or crème fraîche, to serve

truffle oil, for drizzling

VEGETABLE STOCK

1 carrot, chopped

2 celery stalks, chopped

1 garlic clove, peeled

1 onion, skin on, halved

½ teaspoon black peppercorns

1 teaspoon sea salt

Place all the ingredients for the vegetable stock in a large saucepan. Add 1.75 litres (7 cups) water and bring to the boil over high heat. Reduce the heat, then cover and simmer for 1 hour.

Pass the vegetable stock through a sieve, into a large bowl. Set aside and discard the vegetables.

Heat the olive oil in a large saucepan over high heat. Add the fennel, leek and fennel seeds, reduce the heat to medium and sauté for 15 minutes, or until the vegetables are translucent.

Increase the heat and ladle the stock into the saucepan. Add the potato and garlic and bring to the boil, then reduce the heat, cover and simmer for 30 minutes. Remove from the heat and allow to cool.

Using a ladle, transfer the cooled soup mixture to a blender and purée until smooth. Return to the saucepan and gently reheat.

Ladle into warmed serving bowls. Top with a dollop of sour cream, a drizzle of truffle oil and a sprinkling of reserved fennel fronds. Serve immediately.

BEST IN: AUTUMN & WINTER

MAKE IT VEGAN!
Use a dollop of dairy-free sour cream to serve.

Artichoke, basil & baby pea lasagne

SERVES 10

This is a beautiful alternative to traditional lasagne. Using preserved artichokes, rather than preparing fresh ones, makes this dish very quick to assemble. If possible, use artichokes in brine – if yours are packed in oil, be sure to drain them very well. Serve with a simple rocket (arugula) salad, dressed with a balsamic vinaigrette. –VV

olive oil cooking spray

350 g (12½ oz) artichoke hearts in brine

1 teaspoon freshly ground black pepper

375 ml (1½ cups) thickened (whipping) cream (35% fat)

large handful of basil leaves, chopped

500 g (1 lb 2 oz/3¼ cups) fresh or frozen baby peas

800 g (1 lb 12 oz/3¼ cups) firm fresh ricotta

100 g (3½ oz/1 cup) grated parmesan

2 large free-range eggs

1 teaspoon sea salt

375 g (13 oz) packet dried lasagne sheets

450 g (1 lb/3 cups) grated mozzarella

Preheat the oven to 180°C/350°F (fan-forced). Spray a deep 20 cm × 30 cm (8 in × 12 in) baking dish with olive oil.

Drain the artichoke hearts, then cut into slices about 1 cm (½ in) thick. Place in a bowl and sprinkle with the pepper. Drizzle with 60 ml (¼ cup) of the cream, add half the basil and half the peas and gently mix together.

Place the remaining basil, peas and cream in a food processor. Add the ricotta, parmesan, eggs and salt and purée until smooth.

Spread about 1 cup of the ricotta mixture over the bottom of the baking dish, then cover with a layer of the lasagne sheets. Spread half the artichoke mixture over the top, followed by another 2 cups of the ricotta mixture and one-third of the mozzarella.

Top with another layer of lasagne sheets. Spread the remaining artichoke mixture over the top, then most of the ricotta mixture, and another one-third of the mozzarella. Add a final layer of lasagne sheets, then the remaining ricotta mixture and mozzarella.

Cover with foil and bake for 30 minutes. Remove the foil and bake for a further 20 minutes, or until the lasagne is cooked through and the cheesy topping is golden brown.

Remove from the oven and allow to stand for 20 minutes before serving.

BEST IN: SPRING & SUMMER

Asparagus & fennel galette with goat's cheese

SERVES 6–8

This beautiful free-form galette is spectacular fresh out of the oven, as well as cold the next day. It's a perfect one for picnics, or to make in advance. This recipe calls for wholemeal flour, which gives the dish an earthier taste and more hearty feel. If unavailable, just use plain flour instead. –VV

1 tablespoon butter

250 g (9 oz) fennel bulb, cut into wedges 1 cm (½ in) thick

170 ml (⅔ cup) dry white wine

200 g (7 oz) asparagus spears

125 g (4½ oz/½ cup) ricotta

75 g (2¾ oz/½ cup) crumbled goat's cheese

½ teaspoon sea salt

½ teaspoon freshly ground black pepper

PASTRY

150 g (5½ oz/1 cup) plain (all-purpose) flour, plus extra for dusting

150 g (5½ oz/1 cup) wholemeal (whole-wheat) flour

1 teaspoon sea salt

185 g (6½ oz) butter, diced and chilled

60 ml (¼ cup) chilled water

To make the pastry, sift the plain and wholemeal flour into a mixing bowl, returning the wholemeal husks to the mixture. Add the salt and butter. Using your fingertips, rub the mixture together until it resembles breadcrumbs. Add the chilled water and knead together. Turn out onto a floured surface and knead until smooth.

Using your hands, form the dough into a disc. Cover with plastic wrap and leave to rest in the fridge for 1 hour.

Meanwhile, in a large saucepan, melt the butter over high heat. Add the fennel and wine, bring to the boil, then reduce the heat and simmer for 10 minutes, or until the fennel is tender. Set aside to cool.

Preheat the oven to 180°C/350°F (fan-forced).

Cut off and reserve the top 3 cm (1¼ in) from each asparagus spear. Chop the remaining asparagus into 1 cm (½ in) lengths and place in a mixing bowl. Add the ricotta, goat's cheese, salt and pepper and mix to combine.

Remove the pastry from the fridge and place between two sheets of baking paper. Roll out to a circle about 35 cm (14 in) in diameter, and 2 mm (⅛ in) thick. Remove the top sheet of paper and transfer the pastry to a baking tray.

Spread two-thirds of the ricotta mixture onto the middle of the pastry, leaving a 5–6 cm (2–2½ in) border. Arrange the fennel and the reserved asparagus tips around the ricotta mixture, then dollop the remaining mixture over the vegetables. Turn the pastry edges over onto the vegetables.

Transfer to the oven and bake for 40–45 minutes, or until the pastry has browned.

Remove from the oven and allow to rest for 10 minutes, before slicing and serving.

BEST IN: SPRING

Shaved fennel salad with citrus

SERVES 4

Both fennel and citrus really shine in the cooler months, so make the most of their seasonality and enjoy this winter salad as often as you can. –VV

40 g (1½ oz/¼ cup) pine nuts

1 large fennel bulb

45 g (1½ oz) baby rocket (arugula)

250 g (9 oz) celery, sliced on the diagonal

180 g (6½ oz/1 cup) seedless purple grapes, cut in half

12–15 orange segments (see Note)

12–15 blood orange or pink grapefruit segments

2 tablespoons French tarragon leaves

100 g (3½ oz/⅔ cup) crumbled feta

RED WINE VINEGAR DRESSING

90 ml (⅓ cup) red wine vinegar

60 ml (¼ cup) olive oil

½ teaspoon sea salt

¼ teaspoon freshly ground black pepper

Place a small frying pan over medium heat. Add the pine nuts and toast them, stirring constantly, for 3 minutes, or until lightly browned. Remove from the pan and place on a tray to cool.

In a small bowl, whisk together the dressing ingredients. Set aside.

Using a mandoline or very sharp knife, finely shave the fennel, reserving the fronds.

On a large platter, scatter and layer the fennel, rocket, celery, grapes and citrus segments. Drizzle the dressing over. Scatter the reserved fennel fronds over the top, along with the tarragon, feta and toasted pine nuts. Serve straight away.

BEST IN: AUTUMN & WINTER

NOTE: To segment citrus fruit, place the fruit on a chopping board and carefully cut off the top and bottom, using a sharp knife. Sit the fruit on the chopping board, so it has a flat, stable base. Working your way all around the fruit, using downward strokes and following the curved shape, cut away the peel and all the bitter white pith. Working with one citrus segment at a time, and holding the peeled fruit in one hand, cut closely to the white membrane on each side of the segment, to release each fruit segment, reserving any juices for dressing the salad.

MAKE IT VEGAN!
Leave out the feta or use a dairy-free cheese.

Banana blossom & green papaya salad

SERVES 4

Banana blossoms are available fresh from Asian markets pretty much year-round.
Palm sugar adds a lovely sweetness to the dressing. –CG

1 lime, cut in half

1 banana blossom

1 small green papaya, peeled, deseeded
then shaved or shredded

1 carrot, shredded

120 g (4½ oz/1⅓ cups) bean sprouts

2 teaspoons shaved palm sugar

1 small red chilli, finely sliced

40 g (1½ oz/¼ cup) roasted peanuts,
roughly chopped

2 tablespoons crispy fried shallots

small handful of mint, shredded

small handful of Vietnamese mint,
shredded

LIME & GARLIC DRESSING

3 teaspoons shaved palm sugar

1 garlic clove, crushed

2 tablespoons vegan fish sauce

1 tablespoon lime juice

Rub a chopping board and sharp knife with the cut side of the lime. Fill
a bowl with water and squeeze the remaining lime juice into the water,
to make an acidulated water bath to stop the banana blossom browning.

Peel away the outer purple leaves from the banana blossom, until you
get to the pale heart. Discard the outer leaves and any partly formed
bananas. Shred the blossom heart finely and immediately place in the
bowl of acidulated water. Leave to soak for about 30 minutes.

Combine the dressing ingredients in a small bowl, add 100 ml (3½ fl oz)
water and stir until the sugar has dissolved. Set aside.

In a large bowl, combine the papaya, carrot and sprouts. Add the soaked
and drained banana blossom and toss with the palm sugar. Set aside for
15 minutes for the mixture to wilt slightly.

Add the chilli, half the peanuts and half the fried shallots. Add all the
mint. Drizzle with the dressing and toss gently to combine.

Pile onto a serving plate, scatter with the remaining peanuts and fried
shallots and serve straight away.

BEST: ALL YEAR ROUND

ALREADY VEGAN!

Salad of pea shoots & watercress with soy eggs

SERVES 4

Dashi stock powder gives a delightful smokiness to the lightly stained eggs in this otherwise simple Asian-style salad. The eggs will need to marinate for 2–6 hours, but can be prepared in advance. The longer you marinate them, the saltier and more intensely flavoured they will be. –CG

2 tablespoons peanut oil

1 small garlic clove, crushed

50 g (1¾ oz) young pea shoots

50 g (1¾ oz) watercress sprigs

1 small baby bok choy (pak choi), finely sliced, including the stalk

3 baby radishes, finely sliced

roasted black sesame seeds, to garnish

SOY EGGS

2 tablespoons caster (superfine) sugar

1 teaspoon crumbled dried nori

6 free-range eggs, at room temperature

180 ml (¾ cup) light soy sauce

2 tablespoons rice vinegar

For the smoky soy eggs, combine the sugar and nori in a bowl or container just large enough to hold all the eggs. Add 125 ml (½ cup) warm water and stir until the sugar has dissolved. Stir in the soy sauce and vinegar. Transfer 2 tablespoons of the soy mixture to a sealable jar, to make a dressing later on.

Bring a medium-sized saucepan of water to the boil over high heat. Lower the eggs into the water with a spoon and gently stir to distribute the heat evenly. Reduce the heat to a simmer and cook for 6 minutes. Remove from the heat. Run the eggs under cold water, or place in an ice bath until cool.

Under cold running water, or in the ice bath, gently peel the eggs (they will be delicate). Place them in the soy mixture; they should be completely covered in liquid and just floating. To keep them submerged, place a folded piece of paper towel on top.

Cover and refrigerate the eggs for 2–6 hours, gently moving them around several times so they marinate and colour evenly. Remove the eggs from the marinade and store in a sealed container in the fridge for up to 3 days.

To make the dressing, add the peanut oil and garlic to the reserved soy mixture in the jar. Seal and set aside until serving time.

Arrange the pea shoots, watercress and bok choy on a serving platter or plates. Top with the radish. Cut the eggs in half and arrange over the salad. Scatter with black sesame seeds. Just before serving, shake the dressing in the jar until well combined and drizzle over the salad.

BEST IN: SPRING & SUMMER

Steamed choy sum with sesame cashews

SERVES 4

Any wonderful leafy Asian greens will work well here instead of choy sum – try Chinese broccoli, bok choy (pak choi) or mustard greens. This one makes a great side dish on a banquet table, or you can turn it into a meal by serving it with a crispy fried egg and brown rice. –CG

1 tablespoon peanut oil

40 g (1½ oz/¼ cup) raw cashews, coarsely chopped

2 garlic cloves, finely sliced

3 spring (green) onions, finely sliced on the diagonal

1 tablespoon black sesame seeds

1 tablespoon white sesame seeds

1 tablespoon light soy sauce

1 teaspoon sesame oil

2 bunches of choy sum, about 500 g (1 lb 2 oz) in total, trimmed

Heat the peanut oil in a heavy-based frying pan over medium heat. Add the cashews and garlic and cook, stirring, for about 2 minutes, or until the garlic is fragrant and the cashews are starting to lightly brown.

Add the spring onion and cook for 1 minute, then add all the sesame seeds and cook for a further 1 minute, or until the seeds start to 'pop'. Remove from the heat and stir in the soy sauce and sesame oil. Set aside.

Bring a saucepan of water to the boil and set a steamer on top. Cut the choy sum leaves from the stems and add the stems to the steamer. Cover and cook for 2 minutes. Add the leaves to the steamer and cook for a further 1 minute, or until the leaves and stems are just tender.

Arrange the choy sum on a serving platter or plates. Top with the sesame–cashew mixture and serve immediately.

BEST IN: AUTUMN & WINTER

ALREADY VEGAN!

Spiced rhubarb chutney

MAKES 2 × 500 ML (2 CUP) JARS

It's always great to have a savoury use for rhubarb, a vegetable that we tend to treat more as a fruit. If you can wait, let this chutney mature and mellow for three to four weeks before using. It is great with cheese, in sandwiches, or alongside curry and rice. –CG

500 g (1 lb 2 oz) bunch of rhubarb

2 red onions, finely chopped

1 large granny smith or other cooking apple, peeled, cored and chopped

2 teaspoons ras el hanout (Moroccan spice mix)

1 teaspoon finely grated ginger

1 teaspoon cumin seeds

180 ml (¾ cup) malt or apple cider vinegar

165 g (6 oz/¾ cup, firmly packed) brown sugar

ALREADY VEGAN!

Preheat the oven to 180°C/350°F (fan-forced). Wash two 500 ml (2 cup) jars and lids with warm soapy water, rinse well and place in the oven for 30 minutes to sterilise them.

Remove the jars and lids from the oven and leave until cool enough to handle.

Meanwhile, remove and discard any leaves from the rhubarb. Trim the stalks and chop into 2.5 cm (1 in) lengths.

Combine the rhubarb, onion and apple in a large heavy-based saucepan over low heat. Add 60 ml (¼ cup) water and bring to a simmer. Cover and cook, stirring occasionally, for 10 minutes, or until the rhubarb is soft.

Stir in the ras el hanout, ginger, cumin seeds and a good pinch of salt. Pour in half the vinegar and simmer gently for 30 minutes, stirring occasionally.

Dissolve the sugar in the remaining vinegar and stir through the chutney. Simmer gently for 10–15 minutes, stirring often, until the mixture begins to thicken and 'bloop' like lava.

Remove from the heat and ladle into the warm sterilised jars. Seal and set aside to cool.

Label and set aside in a cool dark place for 3–4 weeks to mature. Refrigerate after opening and use within 2 weeks.

BEST IN: SPRING, SUMMER & AUTUMN

Leaves & Leafy Greens

amaranth
leaves
lettuce
nettles
rainbow chard
silverbeet
spinach
watercress
witlof

Spinach & green curry coconut soup

SERVES 4

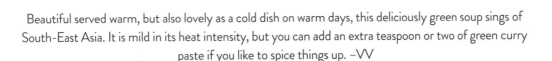

Beautiful served warm, but also lovely as a cold dish on warm days, this deliciously green soup sings of South-East Asia. It is mild in its heat intensity, but you can add an extra teaspoon or two of green curry paste if you like to spice things up. –VV

2 tablespoons vegetable oil

2 tablespoons green curry paste, or to taste

400 ml (13½ fl oz) tin coconut milk

500 g (1 lb 2 oz) bunch of spinach, washed and chopped

1 potato, about 200 g (7 oz), peeled and cut into 1 cm (½ in) cubes

1 teaspoon grated ginger

2 kaffir lime leaves, finely shredded

1 red chilli, finely sliced

ALREADY VEGAN!

Place a saucepan over medium heat. Heat the oil in the pan and add the curry paste. Cook for 30 seconds, or until fragrant.

Pour in about 330 ml (11 fl oz) of the coconut milk, whisking constantly to combine the curry paste.

Add the spinach, potato, ginger and 375 ml (1½ cups) water. Bring to the boil, then reduce the heat. Cover and simmer for 15 minutes, or until the potato is tender. Remove from the heat and allow to cool.

Purée the soup using a hand-held stick blender, or ladle into a food processor and blend for 1 minute, or until smooth. Pour back into the saucepan and reheat over medium heat for about 5 minutes, stirring occasionally.

Ladle into serving bowls. Drizzle with the remaining coconut milk, garnish with the lime leaf and chilli and serve.

BEST IN: AUTUMN, WINTER & SPRING

Fool's pasta with baby spinach

SERVES 4–6

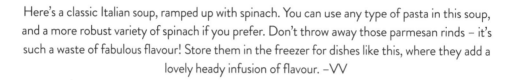

Here's a classic Italian soup, ramped up with spinach. You can use any type of pasta in this soup, and a more robust variety of spinach if you prefer. Don't throw away those parmesan rinds – it's such a waste of fabulous flavour! Store them in the freezer for dishes like this, where they add a lovely heady infusion of flavour. –VV

60 ml (¼ cup) olive oil

1 brown onion, finely diced

1 carrot, finely diced

1 celery stalk, finely diced

1 zucchini (courgette), finely diced

2 garlic cloves, crushed

60 ml (¼ cup) dry white wine

2 bay leaves

1 tablespoon finely chopped parsley, plus some extra parsley leaves, to garnish

1 tablespoon finely chopped rosemary

1 tablespoon sea salt

1 teaspoon freshly ground black pepper

50 g (1¾ oz) parmesan rind

200 g (7 oz/1 cup) podded fresh borlotti beans

115 g (4 oz/¾ cup) risoni, macaroni, penne or broken pasta noodles

125 g (4½ oz) baby spinach leaves

crusty bread, to serve

Pour the olive oil into a large saucepan over high heat. Add the onion, carrot, celery, zucchini and garlic. Stir together, then reduce the heat to medium. Cover and cook for 10 minutes, allowing the vegetables to sweat down.

Remove the lid and increase the heat to high. Add the wine, bay leaves, chopped herbs, salt and pepper. Stir to combine, then bring to the boil.

Add the parmesan rind, borlotti beans and 1.5 litres (6 cups) water. Once bubbling, add the pasta. Partially cover the saucepan and leave to boil for 15–20 minutes, or until the beans are tender and the pasta is swollen.

Turn off the heat and stir the spinach through. Cover and set aside for 10 minutes, or until the spinach has wilted.

Serve in bowls or a soup terrine, garnished with extra parsley, and with crusty bread on the side.

BEST IN: SPRING & SUMMER

MAKE IT VEGAN!
Omit the parmesan rind. If you want an extra umami boost, add a teaspoon or two of nutritional yeast instead.

Ultra-greens soup

SERVES 4–6

It's easy to feel virtuous when tucking into this green veg-packed soup. Here is another beautiful way to use silverbeet stalks, rather than just the leaves. If you'd like a touch of spice, add a splash of sriracha sauce. –CG

600 g (1 lb 5 oz) bunch of silverbeet (Swiss chard)

350 g (12½ oz) bunch of kale

2 tablespoons olive oil

1 leek, white and pale green parts, sliced

2 garlic cloves, crushed

400 g (14 oz) tin cannellini beans, rinsed and drained

1.25 litres (5 cups) Vegetable stock (see page 23)

175 g (6 oz) bunch of broccolini, chopped into bite-sized pieces

olive oil cooking spray

2 tablespoons lemon juice

Greek-style yoghurt, to serve

2 tablespoons sunflower seeds

2 tablespoons pumpkin seeds

MAKE IT VEGAN!
Leave out the yoghurt or use your favourite coconut yoghurt.

Preheat the oven to 160°C/320°F (fan-forced). Line a baking tray with baking paper.

Trim the ends off the silverbeet stalks. Chop the silverbeet leaves, thinly slice the stalks and set aside, keeping them separate. Strip the kale leaves from the stalks. Tear two of the larger leaves into bite-sized pieces and place on the baking tray. Roughly chop the remaining kale leaves and set aside.

Heat the olive oil in a large heavy-based saucepan over low–medium heat. Sauté the silverbeet stalks and leek for 10 minutes, or until softened and starting to colour. Add the garlic and the silverbeet and kale leaves and cook, stirring, until the garlic is fragrant; you may need to add the leaves in batches, waiting for the leaves to wilt so they will all fit.

Add the cannellini beans and stock, bring to the boil over high heat, then reduce the heat to low. Simmer, partially covered, for 10 minutes, or until the vegetables are very tender. Remove from the heat and set aside to cool slightly.

Meanwhile, spread the broccolini on the baking tray with the kale, in a single layer. Spray with olive oil and season with sea salt flakes. Bake for 10 minutes, or until the broccolini is charred and the kale crisp.

Blend or process the soup until smooth, then gently reheat over low heat, if necessary. Stir in the lemon juice and season with salt and freshly ground black pepper.

Ladle into warm bowls and serve topped with the roasted kale and broccolini, yoghurt, sunflower seeds and pumpkin seeds.

BEST IN: AUTUMN & SPRING

Charred baby cos with salsa verde

SERVES 4

Chargrilling lettuce is awesome, adding an element of smokiness, while also bringing out its natural sweetness. For this recipe you can use a chargrill pan, barbecue or even a very hot heavy-based frying pan to char the lettuce.

The tangy green salsa verde is very flexible, depending on what herbs you have on hand, or what flavour you're after – you can simply use parsley, or a combination of other herbs such as basil, chives, oregano or tarragon. –CG

4 baby cos (romaine) lettuces

olive oil, for brushing

lemon wedges, to serve (optional)

SALSA VERDE

large handful of fresh green herbs, finely chopped

1 tablespoon capers, rinsed and finely chopped

1 teaspoon finely grated lemon zest

2 tablespoons extra virgin olive oil

1 tablespoon lemon juice

Combine all the salsa verde ingredients in a small bowl. Season well with salt and freshly ground black pepper, mix well and set aside.

Heat a chargrill pan, barbecue or heavy-based frying pan until very hot. Trim the stem ends of the lettuces, remove any tough outer leaves, and cut them in half lengthways. Brush the cut sides of the lettuce lightly with olive oil.

Working in batches if necessary, cook the lettuce, cut side down first, over high heat for 1–2 minutes, or until lightly charred and starting to wilt, pressing down on the lettuce if you like to assist the charring. Turn and cook for a further 1 minute.

Serve immediately, drizzled with the salsa verde, with lemon wedges on the side, if desired.

BEST: ALL YEAR ROUND

ALREADY VEGAN!

Braised lettuce with broad beans & peas

SERVES 4

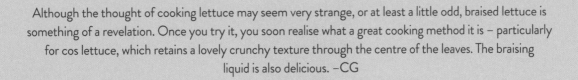

Although the thought of cooking lettuce may seem very strange, or at least a little odd, braised lettuce is something of a revelation. Once you try it, you soon realise what a great cooking method it is – particularly for cos lettuce, which retains a lovely crunchy texture through the centre of the leaves. The braising liquid is also delicious. –CG

250 ml (1 cup) Vegetable stock (see page 23)

20 g (¾ oz) butter

4 spring (green) onions, sliced

500 g (1 lb 2 oz) fresh or frozen shelled broad (fava) beans, blanched and peeled

140 g (5 oz/1 cup) frozen peas, thawed

2 cos (romaine) lettuce hearts, shredded into 2 cm (¾ in) wide strips

handful of mint leaves, shredded

2 teaspoons baby capers

Pour the stock into a small saucepan. Cover and bring to the boil over medium–high heat.

Meanwhile, melt the butter in a large saucepan over high heat. Add the spring onion and cook, stirring, for 1 minute. Add the broad beans, peas and lettuce and cook for 2 minutes, stirring occasionally.

Pour in the hot stock and reduce the heat to low. Cover and simmer for 2–3 minutes, or until the beans and peas are tender, but the lettuce still has some texture.

Stir in the mint and scatter with the capers. Serve immediately.

BEST IN: SPRING

MAKE IT VEGAN!
Swap the butter with olive oil.

Watercress salad with burrata

SERVES 4

Burrata is a fresh Italian cheese, formed into a ball, with a soft creamy centre encased in a shell of mozzarella. You'll find it in Italian delicatessens and good cheesemongers, but you can use fresh mozzarella, labneh or pieces of marinated goat's cheese instead. –CG

100 g (3½ oz) watercress sprigs

3 baby radishes, finely sliced or shaved

1 baby fennel bulb, shaved, fronds reserved

2 baby candy-striped yellow or red beetroot (beets), shaved

4 burrata

edible flowers, to garnish

CROSTINI

8 baguette slices, each about 1 cm (½ in) thick, cut on the diagonal

1 tablespoon olive oil

1 garlic clove

ORANGE MUSTARD DRESSING

2 tablespoons orange juice

2 tablespoons olive oil

1 tablespoon sherry vinegar

1 teaspoon dijon mustard

1 small garlic clove, crushed

pinch of freshly ground white pepper

Preheat the oven to 160°C/320°F (fan-forced).

For the crostini, brush the bread slices lightly all over with the olive oil. Cut the garlic clove in half horizontally and rub the cut sides of the garlic lightly over the bread. Place in a single layer on a baking tray and bake for 10 minutes. Turn the slices over and bake for a further 5–10 minutes, or until lightly golden and crisp.

For the dressing, combine the orange juice, olive oil, vinegar, mustard and garlic in a small screw-top jar. Pop the lid on and shake until well combined. Season to taste with salt and white pepper.

Arrange the watercress and shaved vegetables on individual serving plates. Top with a burrata and scatter with the reserved fennel fronds and flowers. Drizzle with the dressing and serve immediately, with the crostini on the side.

BEST IN: AUTUMN & WINTER

Braised silverbeet & lentils

SERVES 4

If you are lucky enough to have a garden or even just a couple of pots of soil, silverbeet is one of the easiest and most abundant vegetables to grow. When it is in season, you can buy huge bunches of it relatively cheaply. This recipe uses the stalks as well – the secret is to finely slice them and sauté slowly with the onions at the start of the cooking process. This rustic dish is great with crusty bread, or you can add some eggs, cooked your favourite way. –CG

300 g (10½ oz) silverbeet (Swiss chard)

2 tablespoons olive oil

1 red onion, sliced

1 large red bell pepper (capsicum), cut into strips about 1 cm (½ in) thick

2 garlic cloves, finely sliced

200 g (7 oz/1 cup) dried Puy or tiny blue-green lentils, rinsed and drained

2 bay leaves

500 ml (2 cups) Vegetable stock (see page 23)

350 g (12½ oz) mixed cherry tomatoes

2 teaspoons sherry vinegar, or to taste

crusty bread, to serve

Trim the base of the silverbeet leaves and cut the leaves from the stalks. Thinly slice the stalks and coarsely shred the leaves. Set aside.

Heat the olive oil in a large heavy-based frying pan or saucepan. Sauté the onion and silverbeet stalks over low–medium heat for 10 minutes, or until softened and starting to colour. Add the bell pepper and garlic and cook, stirring, for 2 minutes, or until the garlic is fragrant.

Add the lentils, bay leaves, stock and half the tomatoes. Bring to the boil, then reduce the heat to a low simmer. Cover and cook, stirring occasionally, for 25 minutes, or until the lentils are just starting to soften. Add a little water if the mixture is drying out.

Add the silverbeet leaves and the remaining tomatoes. Cook, stirring, until the silverbeet leaves have wilted. Cover and cook for a further 5–10 minutes, or until the lentils are tender.

Remove from the heat, stir in the vinegar and season with salt and freshly ground black pepper.

Serve immediately, with crusty bread.

BEST IN: AUTUMN & SPRING

ALREADY VEGAN!

Spanakorizo

SERVES 4

Black rice adds a healthy twist to this comforting Greek staple, which is traditionally made with long-grain white rice. It also imparts a chewier texture and slightly earthier flavour. This dish is beautiful warm or cold, as a light main meal. –VV

2 tablespoons olive oil

1 brown onion, diced

½ red bell pepper (capsicum), finely sliced

small handful of dill, chopped

small handful of parsley, chopped

2 spring (green) onions, finely sliced

50 g (1¾ oz/¼ cup) long-grain white rice

50 g (1¾ oz/¼ cup) black rice

500 g (1 lb 2 oz) bunch of spinach, washed and chopped

125 ml (½ cup) lemon juice

ALREADY VEGAN!

Heat the olive oil in a large saucepan over medium heat. Sauté the onion and bell pepper for 5 minutes, or until the onion is translucent. Stir in the dill, parsley and spring onion and sauté for a further 3 minutes.

Add the rice and cook, stirring now and then, for 5 minutes, or until translucent.

Pour in 60 ml (¼ cup) water, stirring thoroughly, and cook for a further 5 minutes. Add the spinach, then cover and simmer for 5 minutes, or until the spinach has wilted.

Gently stir to incorporate the wilted spinach into the rice mixture. Season with salt and freshly ground black pepper. Cover with a lid, reduce the heat to low and leave to simmer for 15–20 minutes, or until the liquid is absorbed and the rice is tender.

Remove from the heat and stir in the lemon juice. Cover, and leave to sit for 10 minutes before serving.

BEST IN: AUTUMN, WINTER & SPRING

Spanakopita

SERVES 8–10

The time-honoured Greek spinach and feta pie is given a modern makeover and an extra boost of nutrition with the addition of amaranth leaves. You will find amaranth, with its lovely green leaves with streaks of purple and red, at Asian markets during the warmer seasons. Its deep, rich flavour complements the spanakopita, but if it's difficult to find, you can simply use extra spinach or silverbeet. –VV

500 g (1 lb 2 oz) bunch of spinach

250 g (9 oz/½ bunch) silverbeet (Swiss chard)

250 g (9 oz/2 bunches) amaranth

100 ml (3½ fl oz) olive oil

10 spring (green) onions, chopped

1 brown onion, diced

150 g (5½ oz) feta, crumbled

200 g (7 oz) ricotta

3 tablespoons chopped parsley

3 tablespoons chopped dill

2 free-range eggs, beaten

1 tablespoon ground cinnamon

100 g (3½ oz/½ cup) short-grain white rice

60 ml (¼ cup) melted butter

250 g (9 oz) filo pastry

Wash the spinach, silverbeet and amaranth thoroughly. Trim off any woody ends or roots, leaving most of the stalks intact. Place in a colander, set the colander over a bowl, then cover with a tea towel. Place in the fridge and leave overnight to drain and dry.

The following day, remove the dried greens from the fridge. Preheat the oven to 180°C/350°F (fan-forced).

Finely chop the dried greens and place in a large mixing bowl. Add 2 tablespoons of the olive oil, along with the spring onion, brown onion, feta, ricotta, parsley, dill, eggs, cinnamon and rice. Season with salt and freshly ground black pepper, then gently fold together and set aside.

Add the remaining olive oil to the melted butter and whisk together until combined.

Brush a 25 cm × 35 cm (10 in × 14 in) baking dish, about 5 cm (2 in) deep, with the olive oil mixture. Line the dish with six sheets of filo pastry, brushing each sheet with the oil mixture and laying them on top of each other.

Scoop the spinach filling into the baking dish, spreading it evenly. Layer the remaining pastry sheets on top of the pie, again brushing each one with oil. Trim off any overhanging pastry and tuck the edges in, brushing each sheet with more of the oil mixture.

Bake for 40–45 minutes, or until the pastry is golden. Remove from the oven and leave to rest for 10 minutes, before slicing into pieces and serving.

BEST IN: AUTUMN, WINTER & SPRING

Amaranth with soba noodles & black sesame dressing

SERVES 4

Amaranth leaves have a soft, gentle texture, so take care to not overcook them when stir-frying. Their subtle flavour works well here with the earthiness of the black sesame seeds and soba noodles. If you can't get hold of amaranth, try using mustardy mizuna leaves instead. –VV

250 g (9 oz) dried soba noodles

60 ml (¼ cup) sesame oil

250 g (9 oz/2 bunches) amaranth,
leaves picked

1 teaspoon sea salt

1 teaspoon grated ginger

1 garlic clove, crushed

2 spring (green) onions, finely sliced
on the diagonal

1 red chilli, finely sliced

coriander (cilantro), to garnish

BLACK SESAME DRESSING

3 teaspoons sunflower seeds

100 g (3½ oz/⅔ cup) black sesame seeds

1½ tablespoons grated palm sugar

2 tablespoons tamari

2 teaspoons sake

2 tablespoons olive oil

2 tablespoons lime juice

1 teaspoon sansho pepper (see Note)

ALREADY
VEGAN!

To make the dressing, lightly toast the sunflower seeds in a dry frying pan. Leave to cool, then coarsely grind with the sesame seeds, using a mortar and pestle. Tip into a small mixing bowl. Add the remaining dressing ingredients, stirring with a spoon to combine. Set aside.

Bring a saucepan of water to the boil over high heat. Add the noodles and boil for 4–5 minutes, or until just cooked.

Meanwhile, pour the sesame oil into a large wok. Warm over high heat for 30 seconds, then add the amaranth, salt, ginger and garlic. Toss quickly for 1 minute, or until the amaranth has wilted. Set aside.

Drain the noodles in a colander, then transfer to a large mixing bowl. Add the sesame dressing and gently toss. Add the amaranth mixture and toss to combine.

Transfer to a serving plate, garnish with the spring onion, chilli and coriander and serve.

BEST IN: SUMMER

NOTE: A relative of sichuan pepper, and derived from prickly ash, sansho has a slightly tangy, lemony flavour and delicate tingly, tongue-numbing properties. You'll find it in the Japanese section of Asian supermarkets.

Smoky polenta with garlic & silverbeet

SERVES 4–6

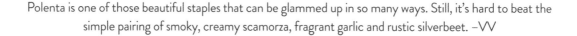

Polenta is one of those beautiful staples that can be glammed up in so many ways. Still, it's hard to beat the simple pairing of smoky, creamy scamorza, fragrant garlic and rustic silverbeet. –VV

150 g (5½ oz/1 cup) fine/instant polenta

125 ml (½ cup) thickened (whipping) cream (35% fat)

150 g (5½ oz) smoked scamorza (see Note), grated

50 g (1¾ oz) butter

375 g (13 oz) silverbeet, leaves washed and roughly chopped

3 garlic cloves, crushed

Pour 1 litre (4 cups) water into a large saucepan and bring to the boil over high heat. Add the polenta, stirring constantly with a wooden spoon. Reduce the heat to a simmer and continue stirring for 4–5 minutes, or until the polenta is thick. Remove from the heat and add the cream and scamorza, stirring until the cheese has melted. Cover and set aside.

Place a large wok or frying pan over high heat and add the butter. When melted, add the silverbeet, garlic and 60 ml (¼ cup) water. Toss constantly for 6–7 minutes, or until the silverbeet has wilted.

Spoon the polenta into a serving dish. Using tongs, top with the wilted silverbeet. Serve immediately.

BEST IN: AUTUMN, WINTER & SPRING

NOTE: Scamorza is an Italian cow's milk cheese, similar to mozzarella, that has been smoked. You'll find it in good cheesemongers and delicatessens. It has a unique flavour that is hard to substitute; the nearest alternative would be a good smoked cheddar.

Grilled witlof with cranberry & pistachio

SERVES 4

Witlof is a delicate vegetable with a crisp texture and nutty, bitter taste. Once grilled, the witlof becomes sweet, while retaining a little of its bitterness. This dish is lovely served alongside the filo cigars on page 60. –VV

2 teaspoons agave nectar

1 tablespoon apple cider vinegar

2 teaspoons balsamic vinegar

1 garlic clove, crushed

2 tablespoons olive oil

4 witlof (Belgian endive/chicory), sliced in half

35 g (1¼ oz/¼ cup) pistachios, roughly chopped

35 g (1¼ oz/¼ cup) dried cranberries

In a small bowl, whisk together the agave, cider vinegar, balsamic vinegar, garlic and 1 tablespoon of the olive oil. Set aside.

Brush the remaining 1 tablespoon olive oil over the witlof halves, using a pastry brush.

Heat a chargrill pan until slightly smoking. Place the witlof halves cut side down in the pan and cook for 4–5 minutes, then turn them over and cook for a further 4–5 minutes, or until nicely charred.

Transfer to a serving dish, drizzle with the dressing and scatter with the pistachios and cranberries. Serve immediately.

BEST IN: AUTUMN, WINTER & SPRING

ALREADY VEGAN!

Pickled rainbow chard stems

MAKES 1 × 500 ML (2 CUP) JAR

Don't throw away those vibrantly coloured stems next time you cook rainbow chard. Pickle them instead! They make a beautiful addition to an antipasto platter, or to accompany a savoury breakfast bowl. –VV

2 teaspoons coriander seeds

250 ml (1 cup) rice vinegar

1 tablespoon agave nectar

½ teaspoon sea salt

½ teaspoon pink peppercorns

6 juniper berries

stems from 1 bunch rainbow chard, washed well and chopped into 2 cm (¾ in) lengths

ALREADY VEGAN!

Preheat the oven to 180°C/350°F (fan-forced). Wash a 500 ml (2 cup) jar and lid with warm soapy water. Rinse well and place in the oven for 30 minutes to sterilise.

Meanwhile, in a small saucepan, toast the coriander seeds over high heat for 1 minute, tossing occasionally so they don't burn. Pour in the vinegar and 125 ml (½ cup) water. Add the agave, salt, peppercorns and juniper berries. Bring to the boil, then reduce the heat and simmer for 3 minutes, or until the agave has dissolved. Remove from the heat and allow to cool for 15 minutes.

Remove the jar and lid from the oven and set aside until cool enough to handle.

Add the chopped chard stems to the jar. Ladle the pickling liquid into the jar, making sure the chard stems are completely covered.

Seal with the lid and leave to pickle in the fridge for 2 days before eating. They will keep in the fridge for up to 6 weeks.

BEST IN: AUTUMN, WINTER & SPRING

Stir-fried watercress & baby tatsoi with baby king mushrooms

SERVES 4

Simple flavours really give shine to two beautiful leafy greens in this stir-fry hero, jewelled with baby king mushrooms. –VV

1 tablespoon sesame oil

2 spring (green) onions, chopped

200 g (7 oz) baby king mushrooms

1 garlic clove, crushed

200 g (7 oz) bunch of baby tatsoi, each head cut in half lengthways and rinsed well

80 ml (⅓ cup) tamari

80 ml (⅓ cup) oyster sauce

300 g (10½ oz) bunch of watercress, washed, stalks left on

1 teaspoon sesame seeds

Pour the sesame oil into a large wok and place over high heat. Heat the oil for 30 seconds, then add the spring onion, mushrooms and garlic. Toss for 1 minute.

Add the tatsoi, tamari and oyster sauce. Cook for a further 3 minutes, or until the greens have wilted, tossing regularly. Add the watercress and cook for a further 1 minute.

Transfer to a serving plate, sprinkle with the sesame seeds and serve.

BEST IN: AUTUMN

ALREADY VEGAN!

Filo cigars with nettles & hummus

MAKES 14

Home-made hummus really sets this dish off, but if you don't have the time to make your own, a good-quality store-bought one will do. Encased in crunchy filo pastry, these cigars are irresistible served warm out of the oven, but are also quite tasty cold. –VV

2 tablespoons olive oil, plus extra
for brushing

1 leek, white part only, finely chopped

650 g (1 lb 7 oz/2 bunches) nettles
(see Note)

handful of dill, roughly chopped

200 g (7 oz) ricotta

100 g (3½ oz) feta, crumbled

1 teaspoon sea salt

14 filo pastry sheets

HUMMUS

400 g (14 oz) tin chickpeas, rinsed
and drained

1 teaspoon smoked paprika

125 ml (½ cup) olive oil

½ teaspoon crushed fresh garlic

1 teaspoon sea salt

1 teaspoon freshly ground black pepper

Preheat the oven to 180°C/350°F (fan-forced). Line a baking tray with baking paper.

Heat the olive oil in a large frying pan over medium heat. Add the leek and sauté, stirring occasionally, for 5 minutes, or until translucent. Add the nettles, then cover and cook for 5 minutes, or until wilted. Set aside to cool, then drain the mixture in a sieve to remove any excess liquid.

Transfer the mixture to a large mixing bowl. Add the dill, ricotta, feta and salt. Season with freshly ground black pepper and stir to combine.

Lay out one sheet of filo pastry. Scoop 2 tablespoons of the nettle filling across the shortest edge of the pastry, leaving a 2 cm (¾ in) border all around the filling. Roll the pasty over the mixture a few times, then fold in the edges. Continue rolling the pastry, brushing the end with a little oil and seal it into a cigar.

Place on the baking tray, seam side down, and brush with more olive oil. Repeat with the remaining pastry and filling, then bake for 10–15 minutes, until the pastry is golden brown.

Meanwhile, place all the hummus ingredients in a food processor. Blend until smooth, adding a little water as you go if the mixture is too thick.

Transfer the hummus to a small bowl and serve with the filo cigars.

BEST IN: SPRING & SUMMER

NOTE: Nettles are a wonderful leafy green that taste like spinach, with a slight peppery taste. Typically available during spring and summer, they are worth seeking out at your local specialty greengrocer. The other option is to go out and pick your own – with care of course to select the correct greens and to avoid getting stung! Silverbeet (Swiss chard) is a great substitute if unavailable.

Seeds
&
Pods

black beans
broad beans
cannellini beans
corn
edamame
flat beans
green beans
okra
peas
snake beans
snow peas
sprouted beans & seeds
wax beans
wing beans

Snake bean, vegetable & tofu curry

SERVES 4

Snake beans, the slightly heartier cousin of green beans, are the star of this dish. They are so named for their length and dark ends that could be mistaken for a snake's head. If you happen to come across the more unusual wing beans with their ruffled frills, add a good handful to your curry near the end of the cooking time.

A Madras curry mix or a French-style curry powder called vadouvan works well here. Serve with steamed rice or quinoa. –CG

2 tablespoons peanut oil

300 g (10½ oz) firm tofu, cut into long rectangles about 2 cm (¾ in) wide

2 teaspoons black mustard seeds

2 teaspoons ground turmeric

1 red onion, cut into thin wedges

2 garlic cloves, crushed

3 teaspoons finely grated ginger

1 tablespoon curry powder

500 ml (2 cups) Vegetable stock (see page 23)

250 g (9 oz) pumpkin (squash), peeled, deseeded and cut into 4 cm (1½ inch) chunks

2 carrots, cut on the diagonal, into chunks

200 g (7 oz) cauliflower, cut into florets

300 g (10½ oz) snake (yard-long) beans, cut into 5 cm (2 in) lengths

250 ml (1 cup) coconut milk

unsalted roasted cashews and pumpkin seeds, to serve

handful of fresh coriander (cilantro), to serve

Heat the peanut oil in a large heavy-based saucepan over medium heat. Add the tofu, mustard seeds and turmeric and cook, gently stirring occasionally, for 2–3 minutes, until the tofu is well coated and lightly browned. Remove the tofu from the pan and set aside.

Add the onion to the pan and cook, stirring occasionally, for 2–3 minutes, or until just tender. Add the garlic, ginger and curry powder and cook, stirring, for 1–2 minutes, until fragrant.

Add a little of the stock and stir to deglaze the pan and loosen any tasty bits stuck to the bottom. Add the pumpkin, carrot and remaining stock and bring to a simmer. Cover and cook for 10 minutes. Stir in the cauliflower and snake beans then cover again and cook for a further 8 minutes.

Stir in the coconut milk and return the tofu to the pan, resting it on top of the vegetable mixture. Cook for a final 5 minutes, or until the tofu is heated through and all the vegetables are tender.

Serve scattered with cashews, pumpkin seeds and coriander.

BEST IN: SPRING, SUMMER & AUTUMN

ALREADY VEGAN!

Green bean & burghul salad with currants & crisp-fried capers

SERVES 8

Toasted seeds and nuts add crunch and texture to this cracked wheat salad, bursting with Middle Eastern flavours. Instead of green beans, you can use flat beans here for a point of difference. —VV

65 g (2¼ oz/⅓ cup) puy lentils or tiny blue-green lentils

225 g (8 oz) green beans, cut into 1 cm (½ in) lengths

175 g (6 oz/1 cup) burghul (bulgur wheat)

75 g (2¾ oz/½ cup) currants

60 ml (¼ cup) ouzo

80 ml (⅓ cup) extra virgin olive oil

3 tablespoons capers, drained

large handful of coriander (cilantro), chopped, plus extra to garnish

handful of parsley, chopped

1 small red onion, finely diced

30 g (1 oz/¼ cup) pumpkin seeds, toasted

30 g (1 oz/¼ cup) slivered almonds, toasted

80 g (2¾ oz/½ cup) pine nuts, toasted

1 tablespoon grated lemon zest

80 ml (⅓ cup) lemon juice

seeds of 1 pomegranate (see Note)

125 g (4½ oz/½ cup) Greek-style yoghurt

MAKE IT VEGAN!
Leave out the yoghurt or use your favourite coconut yoghurt instead.

Fill two medium-sized saucepans with water and bring to the boil over high heat. To one, add the lentils and cook for 25 minutes, or until tender. To the other, add the green beans and blanch for about 1 minute, then remove with a slotted spoon and set aside. Add the burghul to the pan of water and cook for 15 minutes, or until tender. Drain the lentils and burghul and allow to cool, then place in a mixing bowl with the blanched green beans.

Meanwhile, heat a small saucepan over high heat. Add the currants and ouzo and cook for 2 minutes, then transfer to a small bowl and set aside for a little while, for the juices to absorb.

In the same saucepan, heat 1 tablespoon of the olive oil over high heat and add the capers. Cook for 4–5 minutes, stirring constantly until crisp. Set aside.

Add the coriander and parsley to the burghul mixture, along with the onion, pumpkin seeds, almonds and pine nuts. Toss gently to combine. Add the capers, currants and ouzo, lemon zest, lemon juice, pomegranate seeds and remaining olive oil. Combine thoroughly and season with salt.

Transfer to a serving dish, top with dollops of the yoghurt, garnish with extra coriander and serve.

BEST IN: SPRING & SUMMER

NOTE: To deseed a pomegranate, slice off the top and bottom using a sharp knife. Score the skin, through the pith, along each segment. Peel away the skin and pith, to expose the seeds. Using your hands, gently dislodge the seeds into a bowl.

Steamed beans with lemon & pistachio dukkah

SERVES 4

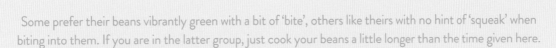

Some prefer their beans vibrantly green with a bit of 'bite', others like theirs with no hint of 'squeak' when biting into them. If you are in the latter group, just cook your beans a little longer than the time given here.

Dukkah is a handy ingredient to have in your pantry, for sprinkling over all kinds of dishes. If you have a nut allergy, replace the pistachios with equal quantities of sunflower seeds and pumpkin seeds. –CG

400 g (14 oz) mixed long beans, such as flat (continental) beans, green beans and yellow wax beans

1 lemon

extra virgin olive oil, for drizzling

PISTACHIO DUKKAH

2 tablespoons sesame seeds

2 teaspoons cumin seeds

2 teaspoons coriander seeds

35 g (1¼ oz/¼ cup) shelled pistachios

½ teaspoon salt flakes

ALREADY
VEGAN!

To make the dukkah, heat a small heavy-based frying pan over medium heat. Add the sesame seeds to the dry pan and toast, stirring often, for 1–2 minutes, or until lightly golden. Tip the seeds into a mortar, or a food processor. Toast the cumin and coriander seeds separately for 1–2 minutes, or until fragrant, then add to the mortar or processor with the pistachios and salt and pound or pulse to a coarse, crumb-like texture. This will make about 60 g (2 oz/½ cup) of dukkah. Any leftovers will keep in a sealed container in the fridge for up to 3 months.

Set a steamer basket over a large saucepan of boiling water. If using flat beans, add them to the basket and steam for 2 minutes. (They will take a little longer to cook than more slender beans.) Add the remaining beans to the steamer and cook for 2–3 minutes, or until cooked to your liking. Transfer to a serving platter.

Shred the zest from the lemon into long thin strips, and cut the lemon into wedges. Drizzle the beans with olive oil and scatter with the lemon zest and a generous amount of dukkah. Serve with the lemon wedges.

BEST IN: SPRING, SUMMER & AUTUMN

Black bean & jalapeño fritters with avocado & corn salsa

SERVES 4

These fritters are especially moreish and really delicious with the avocado and corn salsa. This is a great meal for sharing – throw the salsa, fritters and accompaniments in the middle of the table and let everyone build their own. –CG

12 small tortillas

chopped pickled jalapeño chillies, to serve
(optional)

shredded lettuce, to serve

2 limes, cut into wedges

plain yoghurt, to serve

AVOCADO & CORN SALSA

1 fresh corn cob, husks and silks removed

olive oil, for brushing

1 avocado, chopped

small handful of coriander (cilantro),
coarsely chopped

1 tablespoon pickled jalapeño chillies,
chopped

1 tablespoon lime juice

BLACK BEAN & JALAPEÑO FRITTERS

2 teaspoons olive oil, plus extra for
pan-frying

1 onion, chopped

2 garlic cloves, crushed

1 teaspoon ground cumin

1 teaspoon ground coriander

1 carrot, grated

2 × 400 g (14 oz) tins black beans, rinsed
and drained well

2 large free-range eggs

35 g (1¼ oz/½ cup) fresh wholemeal
breadcrumbs

1 tablespoon plain (all-purpose) flour

1 tablespoon chopped pickled jalapeño
chillies

For the salsa, heat a chargrill pan or barbecue over high heat. Brush the corn lightly with olive oil and chargrill for 10–12 minutes, turning occasionally, until charred and tender. Remove from the heat and set aside to cool, then cut the kernels from the cob. Put the corn in a small mixing bowl with the remaining salsa ingredients and mash together coarsely.

Meanwhile, get started on the fritters. Heat the olive oil in a heavy-based frying pan over medium heat. Cook the onion, stirring occasionally, for 6–8 minutes, or until soft. Add the garlic, cumin and coriander and cook for 30 seconds, or until fragrant. Add the carrot and cook for 1–2 minutes, or until just collapsed. Remove from the heat, transfer to a bowl and set aside to cool.

In a large bowl, coarsely mash the black beans. Stir in the eggs, breadcrumbs, flour, jalapeños and cooled carrot mixture. Mix well.

Heat a splash of olive oil in a large heavy-based frying pan over medium heat. Working in batches, add tablespoonfuls of the bean mixture to the frying pan and cook for 2–3 minutes on each side, or until a lovely crust forms.

Meanwhile, just before serving, warm the tortillas in a large frying pan over medium heat for about 10 seconds on one side only. Stack on a plate and cover with a clean tea towel.

Serve the tortillas as soft tacos, topped with the fritters and salsa with lettuce. Sprinkle with extra jalapeño chilli, if desired. Serve the lime wedges and yoghurt alongside.

BEST IN: SPRING, SUMMER & AUTUMN

Wax beans with candied walnuts & feta

SERVES 6

Using a mix of yellow wax beans and green beans gives this salad a beautiful colour. Walnuts are perfect with this salad, but pecans work well too. –VV

100 g (3½ oz/1 cup) walnut halves

20 g (¾ oz) unsalted butter

55 g (2 oz/¼ cup) sugar

100 ml (3½ fl oz) olive oil

300 g (10½ oz) yellow wax beans, cut in half lengthways

300 g (10½ oz) green beans, cut in half lengthways

125 g (4½ oz) baby spinach leaves

2½ tablespoons wholegrain mustard

80 ml (⅓ cup) apple cider vinegar

2 tablespoons red wine vinegar

1 teaspoon sea salt

1 teaspoon freshly ground black pepper

25 g (1 oz/¼ cup) cooked quinoa

75 g (2¾ oz/½ cup) crumbled feta

Heat a non-stick frying pan over medium heat. Add the walnuts, butter and sugar. Cook, stirring constantly, for 5 minutes, or until the sugar has melted and the nuts are thoroughly coated. Transfer to a tray lined with baking paper and, using two spoons, quickly separate the nuts. Allow to cool.

Heat 2 tablespoons of the olive oil in a frying pan over high heat. Add the beans and cook, tossing frequently, for 2 minutes. Remove from the heat, stir in the spinach leaves and cover for 5 minutes, or until the leaves have wilted.

Pour the remaining olive oil into a mixing bowl. Add the mustard, vinegars, salt and pepper and whisk together. Add the bean and spinach mixture, along with the quinoa. Toss lightly and allow to sit for 30 minutes.

Transfer the salad to a serving dish. Top with the crumbled feta and candied walnuts and serve immediately.

BEST IN: SPRING & SUMMER

MAKE IT VEGAN!
Replace the butter with olive oil and use vegan feta instead.

Green bean salad with grilled haloumi & rum-soaked figs

SERVES 4

The combination of dark rum and figs adds a satisfyingly rich and earthy element to this simple salad of green beans, with haloumi adding some salty pizzazz. This salad is lovely warm or cold. –VV

100 g (3½ oz/½ cup) whole dried figs, cut in half crossways

125 ml (½ cup) dark rum

3 tablespoons honey

500 g (1 lb 2 oz) green beans, trimmed

2 tablespoons olive oil

1 tablespoon balsamic vinegar

1 small red chilli, finely sliced

200 g (7 oz) haloumi, cut into thin strips

60 g (2 oz/⅔ cup) flaked almonds, toasted

lemon zest, to garnish

Place the figs in a small bowl with the rum and honey. Stir to combine, then leave to soak for about 30 minutes.

Heat a saucepan over high heat. Pour in the figs and their liquid. Cook for 1 minute, then add the beans. Cook for a further 1 minute over high heat, then reduce the heat to medium and simmer for 8 minutes, or until the beans are tender.

Remove from the heat and pour in the olive oil and vinegar. Add the chilli and season with salt. Stir to combine and set aside.

Heat a small non-stick chargrill pan until very hot. Add the haloumi and cook over high heat for 2–3 minutes on each side, until golden and nicely grill-marked.

Transfer the bean mixture to a serving plate. Top with the haloumi and almonds, garnish with lemon zest and serve.

BEST IN: SPRING & SUMMER

Smashed edamame with mint & soba noodles

SERVES 4

Typically served salted in their pods as a snack before a meal, young green soy beans are often sold, frozen, labelled as 'edamame'. Try treating them as peas, and smashing them with fresh herbs for a light Japanese-inspired dish. –VV

200 g (7 oz/2 cups) frozen edamame (young green soy beans), in their pods

1 teaspoon finely chopped ginger

2 garlic cloves, crushed

60 ml (¼ cup) lime juice

80 ml (⅓ cup) sesame oil

60 ml (¼ cup) tamari

3 tablespoons black sesame seeds, plus extra to garnish

250 g (9 oz) dried soba noodles

mint leaves, to garnish

Fill a small saucepan with water and bring to the boil over high heat. Add the frozen edamame and boil for 3 minutes, until the pods are bright green. Drain in a colander and run under cold water for 1–2 minutes, until cooled. Using your fingers, gently squeeze the pods to pop the beans into a bowl.

Place the edamame beans in a food processor, along with the ginger, garlic, lime juice, 2 tablespoons of the sesame oil and 2 tablespoons of the tamari. Add the black sesame seeds and pulse for 1–2 minutes.

Place a saucepan of water over high heat and bring to the boil. Add the soba noodles and boil for 4–5 minutes, until just cooked, then drain in a colander.

Transfer the noodles to a large serving platter and drizzle with the remaining sesame oil and tamari, tossing to coat. Add the edamame mixture and continue tossing until well combined.

Garnish with mint and sesame seeds. Serve immediately.

BEST: ALL YEAR ROUND

ALREADY VEGAN!

Pea & cannellini bean mash with basil oil

SERVES 4–6

An upmarket alternative to mashed potato, this lovely mash is made with dried cannellini beans, but if you don't have the time or patience to soak them overnight, simply use tinned beans. When in season, also use fresh peas if you can, instead of frozen. –CG

300 g (10½ oz/1½ cups) dried cannellini beans (see Note)

1 tablespoon olive oil

1 leek, white and pale green parts only, finely chopped

2 garlic cloves, crushed

260 g (9 oz/2 cups) frozen baby peas

125 ml (½ cup) Vegetable stock (see page 23)

BASIL OIL

60 g (2 oz/½ bunch) basil

125 ml (½ cup) olive oil

ALREADY VEGAN!

Soak the dried beans in cold water overnight.

Rinse the beans well, then drain and place in a large saucepan. Add enough cold water to cover the beans by about 5 cm (2 in) and bring to the boil over medium–high heat. Reduce the heat to low and simmer for 45–60 minutes, until tender. Drain and set aside.

Meanwhile, for the basil oil, pick the leaves from the basil stalks and dunk them in a saucepan of boiling water. Drain immediately and refresh in cold water. Drain, then firmly squeeze the water from the leaves. Whiz the leaves with the oil in a blender until smooth and very green. Strain through a fine-mesh sieve, without pressing any of the pulp through. Discard the pulp.

Heat the olive oil in a heavy-based saucepan over medium heat and add the leek and garlic. Cook, stirring occasionally, for 3–5 minutes, or until the leek is soft. Add the beans, peas and stock and bring to the boil. Simmer for 1 minute, remove from the heat and leave to cool slightly.

Purée the bean mixture using a stick blender in the pan, or whiz in a food processor until smooth. Season with salt and freshly ground black pepper.

Serve the mash warm, drizzled with the basil oil. Any leftover basil oil can be stored in a sealed container in the fridge for up to 3 days.

BEST IN: SPRING, SUMMER & AUTUMN

NOTE: Alternatively, you can use two 400 g (14 oz) tins cannellini beans, rinsed and drained, and add them to the pan with the peas and stock.

Snow pea & sesame salad

SERVES 4

This recipe is reminiscent of a beautiful Japanese salad that is normally made with cucumber. Snow peas add great texture and crunch to this refreshing dish. It is lovely paired with vegetarian dumplings or gyoza, steamed rice and a glass of chilled sake. –VV

1 tablespoon white sesame seeds

1 tablespoon black sesame seeds

2 tablespoons white miso paste (shiro miso)

1½ tablespoons tahini

1 tablespoon rice vinegar

2 tablespoons sesame oil

1 tablespoon honey

2 teaspoons chilli flakes

2 spring (green) onions, finely chopped

2 teaspoons finely chopped ginger

300 g (10½ oz) snow peas (mangetout), sliced in half lengthways

1 cucumber, peeled lengthways into strips

3 tablespoons chopped coriander (cilantro) leaves

Heat a small saucepan over medium heat. Add the white and black sesame seeds and toast in the dry pan, tossing frequently, for 1–2 minutes, or until the white seeds begin to brown slightly. Immediately remove from the heat and transfer to a small plate.

In a mixing bowl, whisk together the miso paste, tahini, vinegar, sesame oil, honey, chilli flakes, spring onion and ginger.

Add the snow peas, cucumber and coriander. Toss together gently.

Transfer to a serving bowl, garnish with the toasted sesame seeds and serve.

BEST IN: SPRING & SUMMER

MAKE IT VEGAN!
Replace the honey with agave or coconut nectar.

Braised broad beans with artichoke, peas & dill

SERVES 6–8

Here is a lovely way to make a hero ingredient of the humble broad bean. This is one of my favourite dishes, cooked by my mother for as long as I can remember. Serve warm in winter, or cold in summer with a big dollop of Greek yoghurt. –VV

500 g (1 lb 2 oz) fresh broad (fava) beans

1 lemon

6 large globe artichokes, about 2.4 kg (5¼ lb) in total

500 g (1 lb 2 oz) fresh peas, podded to give about 300 g (10½ oz/2 cups)

1 white onion, finely sliced

6 spring (green) onions, finely sliced

small handful of dill, finely chopped

small handful of mint, finely chopped

small handful of parsley, finely chopped

125 ml (½ cup) olive oil

ALREADY VEGAN!

Preheat the oven to 180°C/350°F (fan-forced).

Bring a small saucepan of water to the boil. Remove the broad beans from their pods, add them to the saucepan and boil for 2 minutes. Drain in a colander, then transfer to a bowl of cold water. Allow to cool for a few minutes, then give each one a gentle squeeze to pop out the inner green bean. Set aside.

Cut the lemon in half and squeeze the juice into a large bowl. Add the lemon halves to the bowl and fill halfway with cold water.

Using a serrated knife, trim the artichoke stems, leaving 5 cm (2 in) of stem attached. Working with one artichoke at a time, trim off the outer leaves by pulling them back and breaking off to expose the tender green heart. Cut one-third off the top, then use a vegetable peeler to clean the base and stem of the artichoke. Cut in half and place immediately in the bowl of lemon water while preparing the remaining artichokes, so they don't discolour.

Add the broad beans to a large baking dish, measuring about 30 cm × 40 cm (12 in × 16 in). Add the artichoke, peas, onion, spring onion and herbs. Drizzle with the olive oil and 125 ml (½ cup) water, season with salt and freshly ground black pepper and mix together.

Cover the dish with baking paper, then a sheet of foil, tucking the edges under to create a tight seal. Transfer to the oven and bake for 30 minutes.

Remove the foil and bake for a further 15–20 minutes, until the artichoke is tender, stirring occasionally, taking care not to break up the artichoke. The braising liquid should have reduced down to about one-third. Remove from the oven and serve drizzled with the braising juices.

BEST IN: SPRING

BBQ corn with chipotle mayo & queso fresco

SERVES 4

Spanish for 'fresh cheese', queso fresco is available at Latin American delis. If not available, substitute mild feta cheese or even Indian-style paneer. Chipotle peppers are smoked red jalapeño chillies, often sold packed in tins in a spicy, tangy tomato sauce known as adobo. The chillies and sauce have a delicious smoky flavour and can be quite hot – you don't need a lot for a good bite of heat. –CG

4 fresh corn cobs, husks and silks removed

olive oil, for brushing

80 g (2¾ oz) queso fresco or feta cheese, crumbled

coriander (cilantro), to serve

2 limes, cut into wedges

CHIPOTLE MAYONNAISE

1 teaspoon dijon mustard

1 free-range egg yolk, at room temperature

1 tablespoon lime juice

250 ml (1 cup) mild olive oil or canola oil

½ chipotle chilli in 1 teaspoon adobo sauce, finely chopped

MAKE IT VEGAN!
Use vegan cheese in place of the queso fresco. To make vegan chipotle mayo, see the aquafaba mayo recipe on page 184, crush ½ small garlic clove and blitz it with the chickpeas, then blend or stir 3–4 teaspoons chopped chipotle in adobo sauce into the mayonnaise at the end.

For the chipotle mayonnaise, whisk the mustard, egg yolk and lime juice together in a bowl. Whisking constantly, add the oil in a very slow trickle, until all the oil is incorporated and the mayonnaise is thick and emulsified. Do not add the oil too quickly or the mayonnaise may separate. Whisk in the chilli and adobo sauce. If the mayonnaise is very thick, it can be thinned with a little warm water. The mayonnaise makes about 300 g (10½ oz/1 cup); you may not need it all for this recipe, but you can refrigerate the remainder in an airtight container, with the surface covered closely with plastic wrap, for up to 5 days.

Heat a barbecue or chargrill pan over high heat. Brush the corn lightly with olive oil and chargrill for 10–12 minutes, turning occasionally, until charred and tender.

Leave the corn whole, or cut the cobs into sections, if you like. Brush the corn with some of the chipotle mayonnaise, sprinkle with the cheese and scatter with coriander.

Serve immediately, with lime wedges and a small bowl of the chipotle mayo.

BEST IN: SUMMER & AUTUMN

Corn tikkis with raita & tamarind sauce

MAKES ABOUT 24 TIKKIS

These tasty corn tikkis are rich in spice and flavour, and a quick way to use up leftover cooked corn, peas and potatoes. If you fancy a little less heat, omit the chilli. The tamarind sauce can be made a few days ahead and stored in a sealed container in the fridge until required; but bring it back to room temperature to serve. –VV

110 g (4 oz/¾ cup) frozen corn kernels, blanched

50 g (1¾ oz/⅓ cup) cooked peas

2 large boiled potatoes, about 600 g (1 lb 5 oz) in total

100 g (3½ oz/1 cup) dry breadcrumbs

1 teaspoon garam masala

½ teaspoon chopped chilli

2 garlic cloves, crushed

½ teaspoon finely chopped ginger

small handful of coriander (cilantro) leaves, finely chopped

vegetable oil, for shallow-frying

TAMARIND SAUCE

1 tablespoon vegetable oil

1 teaspoon ground ginger

1½ teaspoons cumin seeds

1 teaspoon fennel seeds

½ teaspoon cayenne pepper

1 teaspoon garam masala

275 g (9½ oz/1¼ cups) sugar

60 ml (¼ cup) tamarind purée

RAITA

250 g (9 oz/1 cup) Greek-style yoghurt

1 tablespoon lemon juice

1 teaspoon ground cumin

1 small cucumber, grated and strained

To make the tamarind sauce, heat the oil in a saucepan over medium heat. Add the ginger, cumin seeds, fennel seeds, cayenne pepper and garam masala and stir for 1–2 minutes, or until the spices are aromatic. Pour in 500 ml (2 cups) water, then add the sugar and tamarind purée, stirring to combine. Increase the heat and bring to the boil, then reduce the heat and simmer for 40 minutes, or until the mixture coats the back of a spoon. Remove from the heat and set aside to cool completely.

Combine the raita ingredients in a small bowl. Mix together with a spoon, then cover and set aside in the fridge until required.

To make the tikkis, put the corn, peas and potatoes in a mixing bowl and roughly mash using a potato masher. Stir in the breadcrumbs, garam masala, chilli, garlic, ginger and coriander, mixing thoroughly. Season with salt and freshly ground black pepper.

Scoop out two tablespoons of the mixture into your hand and form into a round patty. Place on a lined baking tray and repeat with the remaining mixture.

Heat 1 cm (½ in) of vegetable oil in a large frying pan over medium–high heat. Working in batches, cook the tikkis for 4 minutes on each side, or until golden. Drain on paper towel.

Transfer to a serving plate and serve immediately with the raita and tamarind sauce.

BEST IN: SUMMER & AUTUMN

MAKE IT VEGAN!
Make the raita using your favourite dairy-free yoghurt.

Tempura baby corn with togarashi mayo

SERVES 4

Black sesame seeds add a fabulous taste and visual appeal to a tempura batter. If possible, use fresh baby corn for the best flavour, but if it is unavailable, tinned baby corn is fine. –VV

100 g (3½ oz/⅓ cup) kewpie mayonnaise (see Note)

1 teaspoon togarashi seasoning (see Note)

vegetable oil, for deep-frying

110 g (4 oz/¾ cup) plain (all-purpose) flour, plus extra for dusting

30 g (1 oz/¼ cup) cornflour (corn starch)

pinch of bicarbonate of soda (baking soda)

1 free-range egg, beaten

250 ml (1 cup) cold soda water (club soda)

1 tablespoon black sesame seeds

200 g (7 oz) baby corn (about 18)

2 nori sheets, shredded

In a small bowl, combine the mayonnaise and togarashi. Set aside.

Place a large saucepan over medium heat and fill halfway with vegetable oil. Heat until a cooking thermometer registers 180°C (350°F), or until a cube of bread dropped into the oil turns golden brown in 15 seconds. Line a tray with paper towel and set aside.

While the oil is heating up, sift the flour, cornflour and bicarbonate of soda into a mixing bowl. Add the egg, soda water and black sesame seeds. Using a whisk, gently combine, leaving the mixture a little lumpy.

Place a little extra flour in a shallow bowl. Roll the corn in the flour to lightly coat. One at a time, dip the corn into the tempura batter. Add to the hot oil and fry in small batches for 30–40 seconds, until the batter is crisp, but not yet browned. Transfer to the tray to drain, and cook the remaining corn.

When all the corn is cooked, add the shredded nori sheets to the hot oil and fry for 5–10 seconds. Remove with a slotted spoon and drain on the tray.

Arrange the hot tempura corn on a serving plate. Garnish with the fried nori and serve immediately with the togarashi mayo.

BEST IN: SPRING, SUMMER & AUTUMN

NOTE: Kewpie is a smooth, silky Japanese mayonnaise with a unique taste. It is made with rice vinegar, rather than distilled or white vinegar, and contains more egg than regular mayonnaise, creating a creamier texture.

You will find togarashi seasoning in the Japanese aisle of Asian supermarkets. There are several different varieties, the most common being shichimi togarashi, also known as Japanese seven-spice – a blend of ground dried spices including dried red chilli pepper, nori, sesame seeds and orange peel.

Bean sprouts stir-fry in egg net

SERVES 4

Bean sprouts are sold in supermarkets all year round, but their loveliness is often overlooked, as they are usually used as more of a 'filler' ingredient. Not any more: here's a quick dish that makes a hero of this simple vegetable. Betel leaves can generally be found in Asian supermarkets. These dark green, teardrop-shaped leaves have a unique peppery and slightly bitter taste. If unavailable, rocket (arugula) can be used instead. –VV

2 tablespoons vegetable oil

1 free-range egg, lightly beaten

2 tablespoons sesame oil

250 g (9 oz) packet bean sprouts

6 fresh betel leaves, shredded

200 g (7 oz) punnet sprouted seed mix (such as mung beans, chickpeas and lentils)

¼ small savoy cabbage, shredded

1 garlic clove, grated

1 small red chilli, finely chopped, plus extra, sliced, to garnish

2 tablespoons soy sauce

80 g (2¾ oz/½ cup) peanuts, crushed

2 tablespoons hoisin sauce

coriander (cilantro), to garnish

spring (green) onion, to garnish

Place a non-stick frying pan over medium heat. Pour in the vegetable oil, swirl around and heat for 30 seconds.

Using a tablespoon, drizzle half the beaten egg back and forth across the pan to create a net pattern. Cook for 30 seconds, gently turn over, cook for a further 30 seconds then remove from the pan onto a serving plate. Repeat with the remaining beaten egg.

Place a large wok over high heat. Pour in the sesame oil, swirl around for 10 seconds before adding the bean sprouts, betel leaves, sprouted seed mix and cabbage. Cook for 2 minutes, tossing regularly, then add the garlic, chilli, soy sauce and half the crushed peanuts. Cook a further 2 minutes, or until the bean shoots are cooked through.

Top half of each egg net with the mixture then fold the nets over.

In a small bowl, mix 1 teaspoon water with the hoisin sauce and drizzle over the egg nets. Sprinkle with the remaining crushed peanuts and garnish with the coriander, spring onion and chilli. Serve immediately.

BEST: ALL YEAR ROUND

Pickled okra

MAKES 3 × 500 ML (2 CUP) JARS

Fresh okra, also affectionately known as 'lady fingers', generally appear in summer in good-quality greengrocers. They vary in size, but for these pickles it is best to use small- to medium-sized pods. Pickling them in vinegar adds a lovely sharpness to the okra. Serve them on their own with a drink, or on top of bruschetta for a flavoursome kick. –VV

3 tablespoons sugar

3 bay leaves

1½ teaspoons whole allspice berries

1½ teaspoons yellow mustard seeds

¾ teaspoon fennel seeds

1½ teaspoons coriander seeds

1½ teaspoons chilli flakes

¾ teaspoon black peppercorns

800 g–1 kg (1 lb 12 oz–2 lb 3 oz) fresh okra, gently rinsed, taking care not to break the skins

375 ml (1½ cups) apple cider vinegar

2 tablespoons salt

Preheat the oven to 180°C/350°F (fan-forced). Wash three 500 ml (2 cup) jars and lids with warm soapy water, rinse well and place in the oven for 30 minutes to sterilise.

Remove the jars and lids from the oven and set aside until cool enough to handle.

To each jar, add 1 tablespoon of sugar and a bay leaf. Divide the allspice berries, mustard seeds, fennel seeds, coriander seeds, chilli flakes and peppercorns among the jars, then carefully add the okra, stem side up.

Pour the vinegar and 500 ml (2 cups) water into a saucepan. Add the salt and bring to the boil over high heat. Remove from the heat and ladle into the jars, ensuring the okra is covered.

Seal and label the jars, then store in a cool, dark place for 2 days before eating. Unopened, they will keep in the pantry for up to 6 months. Refrigerate after opening and use within 2 weeks.

BEST IN: SUMMER & AUTUMN

ALREADY VEGAN!

Fruiting
Veg

bell peppers
cucumbers
eggplants
jalapeño chillies
tomatillos
tomatoes

Stuffed tomatoes

SERVES 4–6

A solid favourite that has been cooked in my family for generations. The trick here is to not leave any gaps in the baking dish – hence the potatoes! You can use quartered large potatoes, or unpeeled well-washed kipflers (fingerlings). You can serve this dish as a main, accompanied by a lovely Greek salad. –VV

12 medium-sized tomatoes

1 zucchini (courgette), finely chopped

100 ml (3½ fl oz) olive oil, plus an extra 1 tablespoon

2 brown onions, chopped

4 spring (green) onions, chopped

2 garlic cloves, crushed

small handful of dill, finely chopped

small handful of mint, finely chopped

small handful of parsley, finely chopped

200 g (7 oz/1 cup) long-grain white rice

4 potatoes, peeled and cut into quarters

1 tablespoon tomato paste (concentrated purée)

ALREADY VEGAN!

Preheat the oven to 180°C/350°F (fan-forced).

Using a sharp knife, cut the tops off the tomatoes and reserve. Leaving the tomato skin intact, scoop out the flesh from each tomato using a teaspoon. Roughly chop the tomato flesh. Place in a bowl with the zucchini, along with any tomato juices.

Place the tomato shells in an oiled baking dish and set aside.

Pour 100 ml (3½ fl oz) olive oil into a frying pan over medium heat. Sauté the onion and the tomato and zucchini mixture for 5–6 minutes, or until softened.

Add the spring onion, garlic, dill, mint and parsley and sauté for 2–3 minutes, until fragrant.

Add the rice, stirring frequently for a further 5 minutes, until the rice is translucent.

Stir in 125 ml (½ cup) water, season with salt and freshly ground black pepper and set aside to cool slightly.

Spoon the mixture into the tomato shells, to about three-quarters full, and replace the tops. Place the potatoes into any gaps between the tomatoes in the baking dish.

In a bowl, mix together the extra tablespoon of olive oil, the tomato paste and 125 ml (½ cup) water. Season with salt and freshly ground black pepper and drizzle over the tomatoes.

Transfer to the oven and bake for 45 minutes, lightly covering the dish with foil if the tomatoes are browning too quickly towards the end, and adding a little more water only if required.

Cover with foil and bake for a further 30 minutes. Remove the foil and bake for a final 15 minutes, or until the tomatoes are nicely coloured.

Delicious served warm or cold.

BEST IN: SUMMER

Panzanella

SERVES 4

Large and colourful heirloom tomatoes are the key to this dish — preferably organic ones, for that beautiful sweet flavour. –VV

4 large heirloom tomatoes, about 1 kg (2 lb 3 oz) in total, cut into 1 cm (½ in) thick slices

100 g (3½ oz) assorted baby tomatoes, cut in half

4 mini bell peppers (capsicums), about 180 g (6½ oz) in total, cut lengthways into quarters

8 baby cucumbers, sliced in half lengthways

½ red onion, thinly sliced

3 slices multigrain sourdough, about 200 g (7 oz), cut into 2 cm (¾ in) chunks and toasted

40 g (1½ oz/¼ cup) pitted kalamata olives, sliced in half

7 caperberries, sliced in half lengthways

2 tablespoons white balsamic vinegar

olive oil, for drizzling

BASIL EMULSION

1 garlic clove, crushed

large handful of basil leaves, torn

80 ml (⅓ cup) olive oil

Arrange all the salad vegetables, sourdough chunks, olives and caper berries on a platter.

Place the basil emulsion ingredients in a blender and pulse until you have a smooth sauce. Drizzle over the salad.

Sprinkle with the vinegar and a little more olive oil and season to taste. Serve immediately.

BEST IN: SUMMER

ALREADY VEGAN!

Charred tomatillo tostadas

MAKES 10

There is nothing quite as good as a fresh tomatillo – and the tomatillo salsa is definitely the hero in this Mexican dish. Also referred to as a 'Mexican husk tomato' due to the fine, almost translucent papery husk that encloses it, the flesh of the tomatillo is firm and tastes simultaneously fruity and tart. If tomatillos are not in season, green tomatoes can be used instead. However, don't use tinned tomatillos here – the flavour just won't be the same. –VV

vegetable oil, for shallow-frying

10 small soft tortillas

40 g (1½ oz/½ cup) shaved red cabbage

40 g (1½ oz/½ cup) shaved white cabbage

kernels from 1 fresh corn cob

5 radishes, trimmed and finely sliced

coriander (cilantro), to garnish

hot sauce, to serve

TOMATILLO SALSA

400 g (14 oz) husked tomatillos

1 small white onion, quartered

10 garlic cloves, skin on

1 fresh jalapeño chilli

1 tablespoon vegetable oil

handful of coriander (cilantro) leaves

60 ml (¼ cup) lime juice

Preheat the grill (broiler) to high.

To make the tomatillo salsa, toss the tomatillos in a large bowl with the onion, garlic cloves, jalapeño chilli, oil and a generous pinch of salt. Spread the mixture on a grill tray and grill for 8 minutes, or until charred and tender. Set aside until cool enough to handle. Squeeze the garlic cloves out of their skins and place into a food processor. Add the charred tomatillos, onion and chilli, then the coriander and lime juice. Pulse a few times, until the mixture is chunky and combined. Season and set aside while you cook the tortillas.

Fill a medium-sized saucepan with 3 cm (1¼ in) of vegetable oil and heat over medium–high heat.

When the oil is hot, fry the tortillas one at a time, for 30–40 seconds, until golden brown. Remove using a slotted spoon and drain on paper towel before transferring to serving plates.

Top the tostadas with the cabbage, corn kernels, radish and tomatillo salsa. Garnish with coriander and serve immediately with your favourite hot sauce.

BEST IN: SUMMER

ALREADY VEGAN!

Asian gazpacho

SERVES 4–6

A Spanish classic with a South-East Asian twist! Ripe roma tomatoes really make this chilled soup shine. It is even better eaten the next day, giving all the flavours more time to develop. –VV

1 kg (2 lb 3 oz) ripe roma (plum) tomatoes, cored

1 cucumber, peeled

3 spring (green) onions, plus extra, chopped, to garnish

1 fresh shiitake mushroom

2 tablespoons sesame oil

1 teaspoon chopped red chilli

1½ tablespoons finely chopped coriander (cilantro)

1 teaspoon crushed fresh garlic

1 teaspoon finely chopped ginger

1 teaspoon grated palm sugar

1 teaspoon light soy sauce

30 g (1 oz/½ cup) panko breadcrumbs, toasted

Roughly chop the tomatoes, cucumber, spring onion and mushroom. Place in a food processor. Add the sesame oil, chilli, coriander, garlic, ginger, palm sugar and soy sauce. Blend until smooth.

Transfer to the fridge to chill for at least 3 hours.

When ready to serve, blend the soup again, then ladle into individual glasses or bowls.

Garnish with the panko crumbs and extra spring onion.

BEST IN: SUMMER

ALREADY VEGAN!

Indian-style tomato chutney

MAKES ABOUT 320 G (11½ OZ/1½ CUPS)

If you prefer a slightly chunkier texture for this kasundi-style relish, instead of grating the tomatoes, halve them, squeeze out the seeds and chop them, leaving the skin on. This chutney is great with curry and rice, as a sandwich spread, with hard cheeses, or with the Zucchini, mint and cheese fritters on page 116. –CG

3 teaspoons black mustard seeds

80 ml (⅓ cup) apple cider vinegar

1 tablespoon cumin seeds

1 tablespoon grated fresh turmeric

2 teaspoons grated ginger

4 garlic cloves, peeled

1 kg (2 lb 3 oz) tomatoes

80 ml (⅓ cup) peanut oil

55 g (2 oz/¼ cup) rapadura or brown sugar

1 long red chilli, deseeded and finely sliced

1 teaspoon sea salt

ALREADY VEGAN!

Place the mustard seeds and vinegar in a small saucepan over medium heat. Bring to the boil, then reduce the heat slightly and simmer for about 4 minutes, or until the vinegar is reduced to about 1 tablespoon. Set aside to cool.

Heat a small heavy-based frying pan over medium heat. Add the cumin seeds to the dry pan and toast, stirring often, for 1–2 minutes, or until fragrant. Tip the seeds into a mortar, add the cooled mustard seed mixture, turmeric, ginger and garlic and pound until combined.

Cut the tomatoes in half horizontally and squeeze out the seeds. Grate the tomatoes using a box grater, discarding the skin (which will be left behind as you grate) – it is best to do this on a tray or plate to catch all the juices, to add to the saucepan.

Heat the peanut oil in a heavy-based saucepan over medium heat. Add the pounded spice mixture, along with the grated tomatoes and their juice, sugar, chilli and salt. Simmer, uncovered, stirring occasionally, for about 45 minutes, or until the tomato is reduced to a pulp, the mixture is quite thick and the oil has separated.

Transfer to an airtight container and leave to cool, then store in the fridge where it will keep for up to 4 weeks – or seal the chutney in sterilised preserving jars and store in a cool dark place for up to 6 months.

BEST IN: SUMMER

Red pepper rouille on kipflers with toasted walnuts

SERVES 4

This red pepper rouille is delicious with just about anything! Try it with the Eggplant schnitzels on page 104, the Zucchini, mint and cheese fritters on page 116, or spread on a sandwich. This dish is lovely served as a salad too. –CG

800 g (1 lb 12 oz) kipfler (fingerling) potatoes, scrubbed

2 tablespoons toasted walnuts, chopped

parsley leaves, to serve

RED PEPPER ROUILLE

2 red bell peppers (capsicums), cut lengthways into quarters

1 tablespoon olive oil

3 shallots, chopped

1 garlic clove, crushed

1 tablespoon extra virgin olive oil

freshly ground white pepper, to taste

ALREADY VEGAN!

For the rouille, preheat the grill (broiler) to high. Line a baking tray with foil.

Place the bell peppers, skin side up, on the tray and grill for 10–12 minutes, or until well charred and softened. Transfer to a bowl, cover with plastic wrap and set aside for 15 minutes to sweat, then peel off and discard the skin. Coarsely chop the bell peppers.

Heat the olive oil in a small heavy-based saucepan over medium heat and cook the shallot for 5–6 minutes, or until softened and starting to caramelise. Add the bell pepper along with any lovely juices from the bowl, and the garlic. Cook, stirring occasionally, for 3–4 minutes, until the bell pepper starts to break down.

Remove from the heat and set aside to cool slightly, then whiz the mixture in a small food processor or blender until smooth. With the motor running, drizzle in the extra virgin olive oil and whiz until combined. Season with salt and freshly ground white pepper.

Meanwhile, bring a large saucepan of water to the boil. Place the potatoes in a steamer basket, set it on top, then cover and steam for 12–15 minutes, until the potatoes are tender. Drain and leave to cool slightly, then slice if you like.

Spread about one-third of the rouille over the base of a serving plate or dish. Top with the warm potatoes and remaining rouille, scatter with the walnuts and a few parsley leaves and serve.

BEST IN: SUMMER & AUTUMN

Jalapeños stuffed with roasted-garlic goat's cheese

SERVES 4

These are delicious warm or cold. Depending on the size of the jalapeños, there may be a small amount of roasted-garlic goat's cheese left over, which you can enjoy with a baguette, crackers or baby vegetables. Bonus! –CG

6 fresh jalapeño chillies

2 tablespoons pumpkin seeds, roughly chopped

olive oil cooking spray

ROASTED-GARLIC GOAT'S CHEESE

1 whole garlic bulb

1 teaspoon olive oil

100 g (3½ oz) soft fresh goat's cheese

50 g (1¾ oz) cream cheese, softened

handful of chopped fresh herbs, such as parsley, coriander (cilantro) and/or chives, plus extra to serve

freshly ground white pepper

MAKE IT VEGAN!
Replace all of the cheese in the stuffing with dairy-free cream cheese.

Preheat the oven to 180°C/350°F (fan-forced).

For the roasted garlic goat's cheese, remove any loose papery skin from the outside of the garlic bulb and trim off the top 5 mm (¼ in) of the bulb, leaving the bulb intact. Place the bulb on a square of foil, cut side up. Drizzle the olive oil over the cut surfaces and sprinkle with a little salt. Wrap the foil around the garlic and place directly on the oven rack. Roast for 35–40 minutes, until soft. Remove from the oven and set aside to cool. Squeeze the garlic cloves out of their skins.

Place the cheeses, herbs and roasted garlic in a food processor. Whiz together, scraping down the side of the bowl if necessary, until smooth. Season to taste with salt and white pepper.

Increase the oven temperature to 200°C/400°F (fan-forced). Line a baking tray with baking paper.

Cut the chillies in half lengthways, then scrape out the seeds and membranes using a teaspoon. Fill each jalapeño half with the cheese mixture, to just above the edges of the chillies.

Sprinkle the top of the filled jalapeños with the pumpkin seeds and spray with cooking oil. Place the chillies on the baking tray and bake for 10–12 minutes, or until lightly browned and slightly puffed.

Set aside to cool for 5 minutes, then scatter with extra herbs and enjoy.

BEST IN: SPRING, SUMMER & AUTUMN

NOTE: While roasting the garlic, you can throw in an extra bulb and store it in the fridge to use later in the week, or roast the garlic while you have some other veggies baking in the oven. Alternatively, you can use 8–10 cloves of garlic confit from page 245.

Rainbow slaw with avocado dressing

SERVES 4

Not just great for slaw, the avocado dressing in this recipe is also delicious slathered on sandwiches, dolloped on baked sweet potatoes, or even eaten as a dip with raw vegetable sticks.

To quickly prepare the slaw, use a food processor to shred and grate the vegetables. –CG

300 g (10½ oz) red cabbage, finely shredded

150 g (5½ oz) baby bok choy (pak choi), shredded

1 large carrot, grated

1 small red bell pepper (capsicum), cut into thin strips

1 small yellow bell pepper (capsicum), cut into thin strips

2 tablespoons coarsely chopped smoked almonds or sunflower seeds (optional)

AVOCADO DRESSING

1 avocado

100 g (3½ oz) fresh firm ricotta

125 g (4½ oz/½ cup) Greek-style yoghurt

2 teaspoons lemon juice, or to taste

freshly ground white pepper, to taste

Whiz the avocado dressing ingredients in a food processor until smooth, scraping down the side of the bowl occasionally, if necessary. Season with salt and add a little more lemon juice, if necessary.

Toss the cabbage, bok choy, carrot and bell peppers in a large bowl until combined. Just before serving, toss with the dressing. Serve scattered with the almonds or sunflower seeds, if using.

BEST IN: SPRING, SUMMER & AUTUMN

Roasted eggplant with chipotle & lime

SERVES 4

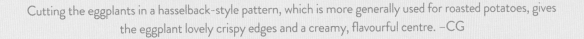

Cutting the eggplants in a hasselback-style pattern, which is more generally used for roasted potatoes, gives the eggplant lovely crispy edges and a creamy, flavourful centre. –CG

2 large eggplants (aubergines), about 500 g (1 lb 2 oz) each

60 ml (¼ cup) olive oil, plus extra for brushing

1 tablespoon chopped chipotle chillies in adobo sauce

zest and juice of 1 lime

60 g (2 oz/1 cup) panko breadcrumbs

handful of coriander (cilantro) leaves, to serve

ALREADY VEGAN!

Preheat the oven to 200°C/400°F (fan-forced). Line a shallow roasting tin with baking paper.

Cut the eggplants in half lengthways and place, cut side down, on a chopping board. Rest a chopstick next to one half, lengthways, on the side closest to you. Make thin parallel cuts at about 7.5 mm (⅓ in) intervals into the eggplant, to about three-quarters of the way through, or until you just hit the chopstick; the chopstick will stop you cutting all the way through. Repeat with the other eggplant halves.

Sprinkle the eggplant lightly with salt, making sure to get salt between the slices. Set aside in a colander, over a bowl, for 20–30 minutes.

Meanwhile, pour 2 tablespoons of the olive oil into a small bowl. Add the chillies in their sauce, along with the lime zest and juice. Set aside 1 tablespoon of the mixture for later.

Rinse the eggplant under cold water and pat dry with paper towel. Place in the roasting tin and brush with extra oil. Transfer to the oven and bake for 20 minutes.

Remove the eggplant from the oven and brush all over, and down into the slits, with the main chipotle mixture. Bake for a further 15–20 minutes, or until browned around the edges and tender in the centre. Remove from the oven.

Switch the oven to grill (broil) mode, or heat a grill (broiler) to medium–high. Combine the breadcrumbs with the reserved chipotle mixture and remaining tablespoon of olive oil. Sprinkle over the eggplant. Grill for 3–4 minutes, until the crumbs are golden.

Serve warm, scattered with the coriander.

BEST IN: SUMMER & AUTUMN

Eggplant schnitzels with buttermilk slaw

SERVES 4

This is great with a dollop of the Red pepper rouille on page 98. Pop the eggplant schnitzels into crusty bread rolls with the slaw and maybe some thick slices of tomato and enjoy as a portable lunch. –CG

2 eggplants (aubergines), about 400 g (14 oz) each, cut lengthways into slices 1.5 cm (½ inch) thick

50 g (1¾ oz/⅓ cup) plain (all-purpose) flour

2 free-range eggs

60 g (2 oz/1 cup) panko breadcrumbs

2 tablespoons chia seeds

25 g (1 oz/¼ cup) grated parmesan

handful of parsley, chopped

2 tablespoons olive oil

40 g (1½ oz) butter

BUTTERMILK SLAW

1 garlic clove, crushed

½ teaspoon salt

180 ml (¾ cup) buttermilk

80 g (2¾ oz/⅓ cup) sour cream

1 tablespoon lime juice

2 teaspoons rapadura sugar or brown sugar

300 g (10½ oz) white cabbage, finely shredded

1 carrot, grated

1 granny smith apple, cut into thin strips

1 small red bell pepper (capsicum), cut into thin strips

large handful of coriander (cilantro) leaves

Sprinkle the eggplant slices lightly with salt and leave in a colander set over a bowl for 30 minutes. Rinse well and pat dry with paper towel.

Place the flour and some freshly ground black pepper in a zip-lock bag and shake to combine. Whisk the eggs in a shallow bowl. Combine the breadcrumbs, chia seeds, parmesan and parsley in another shallow bowl.

Add the eggplant, a few slices at a time, to the zip-lock bag and shake to coat in the flour mixture, shaking off the excess. Dip the eggplant in the egg, allowing the excess to drip off, and then finally press into the crumb mixture. Repeat with the remaining eggplant.

For the slaw, mash together the garlic and salt to form a paste, then place in a screw-top jar. Add the buttermilk, sour cream, lime juice and sugar. Seal the jar and shake the dressing until combined. Season to taste with salt and freshly ground black pepper.

In a large bowl, combine the cabbage, carrot, apple and bell pepper. Stir in half the dressing and set aside for 10 minutes. Add the coriander, and a little more dressing if you think it's needed, and toss to combine.

Heat the olive oil and butter in a large heavy-based frying pan over medium heat. Working in batches, cook the eggplant schnitzels for 2–3 minutes on each side, until golden and cooked through, adding a little extra oil and butter to the pan if necessary.

Serve warm with the slaw, with the remaining dressing for those who may like a bit extra.

BEST IN: SPRING, SUMMER & AUTUMN

Miso eggplant & soba noodle salad

SERVES 4

Steaming the eggplant before roasting helps the cooking process along, and gives it a wonderful texture. The shiro miso dressing is delicious and can be used to dress up a plain lettuce salad, and is great on tomatoes. –CG

3 long slender purple Japanese eggplants (aubergines), about 500 g (1 lb 2 oz) in total, cut into 2 cm (¾ in) thick rounds

140 g (5 oz/1 cup) frozen podded edamame (young green soy beans)

150 g (5½ oz) sugar snap peas

180 g (6½ oz) dried soba noodles

½ teaspoon sesame oil

150 g (5½ oz) snow peas (mangetout), finely sliced lengthways

1 teaspoon toasted white sesame seeds

1 teaspoon toasted black sesame seeds

SHIRO MISO DRESSING

80 g (2¾ oz/¼ cup) white miso paste (shiro miso)

1 tablespoon coconut sugar

2 tablespoons mirin

2 teaspoons light soy sauce

ALREADY VEGAN!

Preheat the oven to 180°C/350°F (fan-forced). Line a baking tray with baking paper.

Bring a large saucepan of water to the boil and set a steamer on top. Place the eggplant in the steamer, then cover and steam for 5 minutes, or until tender.

Meanwhile, in a small bowl, whisk the dressing ingredients together until the sugar has dissolved.

Keeping the steamer basket handy, transfer the eggplant to a large mixing bowl and toss with 2 tablespoons of the miso dressing. Place the slices on the baking tray in a single layer, then bake for 15–20 minutes, or until the sauce starts to caramelise and the eggplant browns slightly. Remove from the oven, brush lightly with a little more of the dressing and set aside to cool a little.

Meanwhile, steam the edamame for 4–5 minutes, or until tender. Refresh in iced water. Steam the sugar snap peas for 1 minute, then refresh in iced water. Drain the edamame and peas and set aside.

Bring another large saucepan of water to a rapid boil (or just use the same pan you used for steaming the veggies). Add the noodles and boil for 4 minutes, or until just tender. Drain, rinse the noodles well under cold water, then drain again. Transfer to a large mixing bowl.

Stir the sesame oil and 1 tablespoon of water into the remaining miso dressing, to thin it down to a smooth pouring consistency. Add the snow peas and steamed vegetables to the noodles and combine gently. Just before serving, mix through two-thirds of the dressing.

Transfer to a serving plate, top with the eggplant, scatter with the sesame seeds and serve drizzled with the remaining dressing.

BEST IN: SUMMER & AUTUMN

Sichuan eggplant

SERVES 4

This dish has a lovely sauce, allowing the eggplant to absorb lots of flavoursome liquid, resulting in one tasty meal. Chinkiang vinegar is a black Chinese rice vinegar that is pretty widely available these days, but rice wine vinegar works just as well.

Typically used in Sichuan-style cooking, doubanjiang paste is made from fermented broad beans and soy beans, and has a complex, unique spicy flavour. You'll find it in the chilli paste section of most Asian grocers, sometimes under the name 'Sichuan hot bean paste'. –VV

2 tablespoons salt

4 long slender purple Japanese or Chinese eggplants (aubergines), about 700 g (1 lb 9 oz) in total

60 ml (¼ cup) rice wine vinegar

60 ml (¼ cup) Shaoxing rice wine

2 teaspoons light soy sauce

1 tablespoon grated palm sugar

1 tablespoon Chinkiang vinegar (Chinese black vinegar)

60 ml (¼ cup) vegetable oil

4 garlic cloves, crushed

1 tablespoon finely chopped ginger

4 spring (green) onions, cut into 3 cm (1¼ in) batons

2 tablespoons doubanjiang paste

coriander (cilantro) sprigs, to garnish

Add the salt to a medium-sized bowl of water. Trim the tops off the eggplants. Slice the eggplants lengthways into quarters, then into 3 cm (1½ in) lengths. Add to the bowl of water and leave to soak for 10 minutes, then rinse and drain.

In a small saucepan, bring the rice wine vinegar to a simmer over medium heat. Remove from the heat and stir in the Shaoxing rice wine, soy sauce, sugar and Chinkiang vinegar.

Place a wok over high heat and pour in the vegetable oil. Reduce the heat to medium, add the eggplant and cook, tossing often, for 5–6 minutes, or until browned. Increase the heat and add the garlic, ginger and spring onion. Cook for 30 seconds, tossing constantly.

Stir in the doubanjiang paste and cook for a further 30 seconds, then pour in the vinegar mixture. Toss constantly for 2 minutes, coating all the eggplant pieces.

Transfer to a serving plate, garnish with coriander and serve.

BEST IN: SUMMER & AUTUMN

ALREADY VEGAN!

Baba ghanoush & tomato salad with quick flatbreads

SERVES 4

If you enjoy your baba ghanoush extra smoky, cook it directly over a flame or open barbecue. This delicious dip partners very well with the zesty and fresh tomato salad and easy flatbreads. If you do decide to go with the smoky option on the eggplant, why not cook your flatbreads on the hotplate of your barbecue while you're at it? –CG

BABA GHANOUSH

1 large eggplant (aubergine), about 500 g (1 lb 2 oz)

1 tablespoon lemon juice, or to taste

3 teaspoons hulled tahini

1 small garlic clove, crushed

handful of mint leaves, shredded

TOMATO SALAD

350 g (12½ oz) mixed small or cherry tomatoes, or 3 medium-sized tomatoes

3 spring (green) onions, finely sliced

handful of mint leaves, shredded

1 tablespoon lime juice

1 small red chilli, finely sliced (optional)

QUICK FLATBREADS

250 g (9 oz/1⅔ cups) self-raising flour, plus extra for dusting

1 teaspoon sea salt flakes

1 teaspoon baking powder

250 g (9 oz/1 cup) plain yoghurt, approximately

Preheat the oven to 160°C/320°F (fan-forced). Line a baking tray with baking paper.

For the baba ghanoush, pierce the eggplant all over with a fork. Heat a heavy-based frying pan, chargrill pan or barbecue hotplate to medium–high heat. Cook the eggplant, turning occasionally, for 10–15 minutes, or until well charred in spots. Alternatively, you can cook the eggplant on a wire rack over a gas stovetop flame.

Transfer the eggplant to the baking tray and bake for 15–20 minutes, or until tender. (For a smokier eggplant, continue cooking on the stovetop or barbecue until tender.)

Set the eggplant aside until cool enough to handle. Cut in half and scoop out the flesh, discarding the skin. Either chop the flesh roughly for a chunky dip, or whiz in a food processor with the lemon juice, tahini and garlic until smooth. Stir in the mint and season to taste. Cover and refrigerate until required; the baba ghanoush will be good for a day or two.

For the tomato salad, slice, halve or quarter the tomatoes, depending on their size. Combine in a bowl with the spring onion, mint, lime juice and chilli, if using. Set aside for an hour or so, for the flavours to develop.

For the flatbreads, combine the flour, salt and baking powder in a large bowl. Add most of the yoghurt and mix until a soft dough forms. If it is a bit dry, add the remaining yoghurt. Knead gently until combined. Cover and rest for 10 minutes.

Turn the dough out onto a lightly floured surface and divide into six equal portions. Roll each portion into a circle, about 18 cm (7 in) in diameter, trying not to add too much additional flour as you roll.

Heat a large heavy-based frying pan over medium heat. Cook the breads, one at a time, for 1–2 minutes on each side, or until nicely browned in spots and cooked through; the second side will start to puff up slightly. Place on a clean tea towel and cover while cooking the remaining breads.

Serve the warm flatbreads with the tomato salad and baba ghanoush.

BEST IN: SUMMER & AUTUMN

Sweet & sour cucumber

SERVES 4–6

At my house, this classic salad would make an appearance at every barbecue when I was growing up. My beautiful mum would always serve it in a gorgeous 1960s stainless-steel bowl with curved sides that folded in like a wave.

This recipe has been updated slightly with coconut sugar and shallots. To get the presentation just right, run a fork down the peeled length of the cucumber to make little indentations all the way along before you slice it. –CG

40 g (1½ oz/¼ cup) coconut sugar or brown sugar

60 ml (¼ cup) apple cider vinegar or malt vinegar

1 long cucumber

2 shallots, finely sliced

ALREADY VEGAN!

Combine the sugar and vinegar in a bowl and stir until the sugar has dissolved.

Peel the cucumber lengthways, leaving some skin on – the cucumber will look striped. Run a fork down the peeled sections of the cucumber. Slice thinly into rounds, then add to the vinegar mixture with the shallot and a very generous grind of black pepper. Stir well.

Set aside for at least 30 minutes for the flavours to develop.

Any leftovers will keep in a sealed container in the fridge for up to 7 days.

BEST IN: SUMMER & AUTUMN

Spicy avocado & watermelon salad with mint & jalapeño chilli

SERVES 4

Mixing both pink and yellow watermelon makes for a gloriously coloured summer salad. If you can't find the yellow variety, just use pink watermelon. This salad works well with Mexican dishes such as tostadas. –VV

2 tablespoons grated palm sugar

60 ml (¼ cup) balsamic vinegar

½ small fresh jalapeño chilli, finely chopped

500 g (1 lb 2 oz) pink seedless watermelon, chilled

500 g (1 lb 2 oz) yellow seedless watermelon, chilled

½ red onion, finely sliced

200 g (7 oz/1 cup) finely sliced feta

1 avocado, diced

100 g (3½ oz) snow pea (mangetout) shoots

1 long red chilli, finely sliced

4 finger limes (see Note)

60 ml (¼ cup) lime juice

salt flakes, for sprinkling

Place the palm sugar, vinegar and jalapeño chilli in a small saucepan over high heat. Bring to the boil, stirring constantly, then reduce the heat and simmer for 5 minutes, or until nice and thick. Set aside to cool slightly.

Cut the melons into 1 cm (½ in) thick slices, then into wedges. Remove the outer rind.

Arrange the melon wedges on a large platter, along with the onion, feta, avocado, snow pea shoots, chilli and the 'caviar' from the finger limes. Drizzle the lime juice over the salad, followed by the balsamic glaze.

Sprinkle with salt flakes and serve immediately.

BEST IN: SUMMER

NOTE: Commonly referred to as 'lime caviar', the finger lime is a native Australian fruit typically grown in warm, subtropical climates such as southern Queensland. To remove the finger lime caviar, simply cut the lime in half horizontally and gently squeeze the lime to push the caviar out. If you are unable to find finger limes, you can peel and segment a standard lime as an alternative.

MAKE IT VEGAN!
Leave out the feta or replace it with a non-dairy cheese.

Squash

baby squash

pumpkin

spaghetti squash

zucchini

Zucchini, mint & cheese fritters

SERVES 4

These fritters are delightful as a breakfast dish, lunch or light main meal. They are so moreish that you may even find yourself making them into bite-sized fritters and serving them as snacks. –CG

3 zucchini (courgettes), about 500 g (1 lb 2 oz) in total

185 g (6½ oz/¾ cup) crumbled fresh firm ricotta

125 ml (½ cup) buttermilk

2 large free-range eggs, separated

110 g (4 oz/¾ cup) self-raising flour

1 teaspoon baking powder

½ teaspoon ground cumin

½ teaspoon ground turmeric

100 g (3½ oz/⅔ cup) crumbled feta

3 spring (green) onions, sliced

handful of fresh mint leaves, shredded

2 garlic cloves, crushed

olive oil, for pan-frying

100 g (3½ oz) rocket (arugula), baby spinach or salad leaves

Indian-style tomato chutney (see page 97), to serve

plain yoghurt, to serve

Coarsely grate the zucchini. Place in a sieve, squeeze out as much liquid as you can, then set aside.

Put the ricotta, buttermilk and egg yolks in a large bowl, stirring until combined. Sift the flour, baking powder and spices over the ricotta mixture, then stir through until just combined. Stir in the zucchini, feta, spring onion, mint and garlic. Season with salt and freshly ground black pepper.

Using an electric mixer on medium speed, beat the egg whites with a pinch of salt until stiff peaks form. Using a large spoon or spatula, gently fold the egg whites into the batter in two batches.

Heat a large non-stick frying pan over low–medium heat. Drizzle a little olive oil into the pan. Working in batches, add 80 ml (⅓ cup) measures of the mixture to the pan and cook for 3–4 minutes on each side, or until puffed, well browned, and just cooked through.

Serve the fritters warm, with the leafy greens, chutney and yoghurt.

BEST IN: SPRING & SUMMER

Zucchini 'noodle' salad with lime & sesame dressing

SERVES 4

For maximum effect, use different kinds of zucchini if you can – including the widely available green variety, or the light green Lebanese zucchini, or yellow zucchini. –CG

2 zucchini (courgettes)

1 carrot

200 g (7 oz) mixed cherry tomatoes

2 tablespoons cashews or almonds, toasted

large handful of coriander (cilantro) leaves

handful of mint leaves

1 tablespoon sesame seeds, toasted

LIME & SESAME DRESSING

3 teaspoons coconut sugar

2 tablespoons peanut oil

1 tablespoon lime juice

1 teaspoon sesame oil

2 teaspoons light soy sauce

Combine all the dressing ingredients in a screw-top jar. Seal and shake until combined.

Thinly slice the zucchini and carrot lengthways, then cut into long, thin strands – or use a spiral cutter or julienne peeler, if you have one. Place in a large bowl.

Slice or halve the tomatoes, depending on their size. Add to the bowl, along with the nuts, herbs and sesame seeds.

Drizzle the dressing over and toss to combine. Serve straight away, or let the salad sit in the fridge for an hour or two to allow the flavours to infuse.

BEST IN: SPRING & SUMMER

ALREADY VEGAN!

Squash with lemon & basil

SERVES 4

Choose a selection of in-season summer squash varieties for this recipe, such as baby zucchini, white/Lebanese zucchini, button or baby yellow squash, or the more common green zucchini. When you cook squash in the manner below, the texture becomes deliciously unctuous, with lovely flavour coming from the caramelisation. Great as a side, this dish is wonderful served warm, as well as at room temperature. –CG

2½ tablespoons olive oil

2 garlic cloves, thinly sliced

700 g (1 lb 9 oz) mixed summer squash, such as baby zucchini (courgette), green zucchini, white/Lebanese zucchini, baby (pattypan) squash, cut into bite-sized pieces

1 lemon

handful of basil leaves

ALREADY VEGAN!

Heat the oil in a large heavy-based frying pan over medium heat. Add the garlic and cook, stirring occasionally, for 2–3 minutes until golden. Remove with a slotted spoon and drain on paper towel.

Increase the heat to medium–high and add all the squash to the pan. Cook, turning the squash occasionally, for 10–12 minutes, or until well browned on all sides and very tender.

Cut long thin shreds of zest from the lemon and set aside. Cut the lemon into quarters and squeeze two of them over the squash. Season with salt and pepper.

Serve the squash warm or at room temperature, scattered with the lemon zest, fried garlic and basil, with the remaining lemon wedges alongside.

BEST IN: SPRING & SUMMER

Mexican zucchini, peas & corn salad

SERVES 4

Substantial enough to be served on its own as a main, this salad is also fantastic as a side dish with tostadas or tacos, and perhaps a nip of mezcal! –VV

200 g (7 oz/1 cup) dried black-eyed peas

200 g (7 oz/1 cup) Puy lentils (tiny blue-green lentils), rinsed

olive oil cooking spray

1 fresh corn cob, husk and silks removed

2 white zucchini (courgettes), thinly sliced lengthways, using a peeler

2 green zucchini (courgettes), cut on the diagonal into 1 cm (½ in) thick slices

1 small red onion, finely diced

1 small red bell pepper (capsicum), finely diced

1 green chilli, deseeded and chopped

4 tablespoons chopped coriander (cilantro), plus extra to garnish

75 g (2¾ oz/½ cup) currants

sour cream, to serve

crispy tortilla strips, to garnish

LIME & CAYENNE DRESSING

60 ml (¼ cup) extra virgin olive oil

1 teaspoon sea salt

1 teaspoon freshly ground black pepper

1 tablespoon ground cumin

1 small garlic clove, crushed

pinch of cayenne pepper

1 tablespoon lime juice, or to taste

BEST IN: SPRING & SUMMER

Fill two medium-sized saucepans three-quarters full of water and bring to the boil.

Add the black-eyed peas to one saucepan and cook for 30 minutes, or until done. Meanwhile, add the lentils to the other saucepan, reduce the heat to a simmer and cook for 15–20 minutes, or until tender.

As soon as the peas and lentils are cooked, strain separately in a colander, rinse under running water and drain. Add both to the same large bowl and set aside.

Heat a large chargrill pan over high heat. Spray with olive oil. Add the whole corn cob and some of the zucchini. Cook for 3 minutes, or until the zucchini is charred, then turn the zucchini and corn and cook for another 3 minutes. Transfer the charred zucchini to a tray to cool slightly and turn the corn again. Add some more zucchini to the pan, cooking it in the same way. Once the corn is charred all over, remove from the pan and leave to cool completely, then cut off the kernels using a sharp knife.

Add the zucchini and corn to the peas and lentils, along with the onion, bell pepper, chilli, coriander and currants.

In a small bowl, whisk together the dressing ingredients. Drizzle over the salad and gently mix through. This salad is best served fresh, but can be made a day ahead and kept in the fridge.

Serve topped with sour cream, extra coriander and crispy tortilla strips.

MAKE IT VEGAN!
Serve with a nice dollop of vegan sour cream.

Sautéed zucchini with mint & pine nuts

SERVES 4

A perfect sharing dish for the warmer months, this one is also wonderful tossed through cooked pasta or served as a cold salad. –VV

2 green zucchini (courgettes)

2 yellow zucchini (courgettes)

1 tablespoon butter

40 g (1½ oz/¼ cup) pine nuts

10 snow peas (mangetout), cut into thin strips

25 g (1 oz/¼ cup) shaved parmesan

handful of mint leaves, to garnish

lemon zest, to garnish

LEMON MUSTARD DRESSING

60 ml (¼ cup) lemon juice

1 teaspoon lemon zest

1 teaspoon honey

1 teaspoon dijon mustard

1 teaspoon wholegrain mustard

½ teaspoon sea salt

60 ml (¼ cup) olive oil

BEST IN: SPRING & SUMMER

Combine all the dressing ingredients in a small bowl and whisk until combined. Set aside.

Using a mandoline or very sharp knife, thinly slice the zucchini.

Heat a heavy-based frying pan over medium heat. Melt the butter, add the zucchini and sauté for 3 minutes. Add the pine nuts and cook for a further 1 minute.

Transfer to a serving bowl, then gently mix the snow peas through, using a spoon.

Give the dressing another quick whisk, then gently mix through the zucchini with the parmesan.

Garnish with the mint and lemon zest and serve.

MAKE IT VEGAN!
Replace the butter with oil and parmesan with a hard vegan cheese and use sugar, agave syrup or coconut nectar instead of honey to sweeten the dressing.

Crumbed zucchini batons with truffle aioli

SERVES 4

These batons make for the perfect starter or afternoon treat in the sun with a glass of rosé. Whole baby zucchini also work really well for this recipe. –VV

vegetable oil, for deep-frying

80 g (2¾ oz/1⅓ cups) panko breadcrumbs

75 g (2¾ oz/¾ cup) finely grated parmesan

1 teaspoon sea salt flakes

2 free-range eggs

3 medium-sized zucchini (courgettes), cut into batons 5 cm (2 in) long and 1.5 cm (½ in) wide

TRUFFLE AIOLI

2 egg yolks

3 garlic cloves, crushed

½ teaspoon sea salt flakes

1 tablespoon vegetable oil

250 ml (1 cup) olive oil

60 ml (¼ cup) truffle oil

For the aioli, place the egg yolks, garlic, salt and vegetable oil in a food processor. Blend for 30 seconds, or until incorporated. Scrape down the sides of the bowl, then blend again, slowly adding the olive oil in a thin steady stream, followed by the truffle oil, and blend until the mixture emulsifies. Set aside.

Fill a medium-sized, heavy-based frying pan with 6 cm (2½ in) of vegetable oil. Heat over medium heat until a cooking thermometer registers 180°C (350°F), or until a cube of bread dropped into the oil turns golden brown in 15 seconds.

Meanwhile, line a tray with baking paper. Place the panko crumbs, parmesan and salt in a bowl and mix together with a spoon. In another bowl, whisk the eggs.

One by one, dip the zucchini batons in the egg, then the crumb mixture. Press the crumbs onto the zucchini to coat completely, then place the batons on the lined tray.

When the oil is heated, fry the batons in batches, gently turning now and then, for 3–4 minutes, until golden brown. Using a slotted spoon, transfer to paper towels to drain briefly.

Serve immediately, with the truffle aioli.

BEST IN: SPRING & SUMMER

Zucchini, mango & green bean salad

SERVES 4–6

Here's a fresh take on traditional Vietnamese flavours. Fresh pineapple also stands in brilliantly in this salad if you don't have mango. –VV

400 g (14 oz) green beans, trimmed and cut in half lengthways

2 green or yellow zucchini (courgettes)

1 mango, peeled and sliced into thin strips

handful of coriander (cilantro) leaves

LIME & CHILLI DRESSING

1 teaspoon salt

2 garlic cloves, crushed

½ teaspoon chilli flakes

1½ tablespoons grated palm sugar

1½ tablespoons light soy or vegan fish sauce

1 tablespoon lime juice

1 spring (green) onion, finely sliced

Fill a large saucepan with water and bring to the boil. Blanch the beans for 1 minute, then remove with a slotted spoon and transfer to a colander. Refresh under cold running water until cooled. Leave to drain until dry, then place in a large serving bowl.

To make the dressing, use a mortar and pestle to grind the salt, garlic and chilli flakes into a paste. Add the palm sugar, soy sauce, lime juice and spring onion. Combine with a spoon.

Using a mandoline, peeler or very sharp knife, slice the zucchini lengthways into long strips. Add to the beans, along with the mango, coriander and the dressing.

Gently toss and serve immediately.

BEST IN: SPRING & SUMMER

ALREADY VEGAN!

Spaghetti squash patties with sriracha mayo

SERVES 4

Baking spaghetti squash magically turns the firm yellow flesh into spaghetti-like ribbons or strands, which make a great pasta alternative whenever you'd like a lower-carb meal. Deep-frying the squash strands makes for an incredible-looking patty, highlighting all the glorious 'spaghetti' strands and giving a great amount of crunch. If you are opting for a healthier approach, shallow-frying works well too, although the crunch won't be quite as pronounced. –VV

1 spaghetti squash, about 1.5 kg (3 lb 5 oz)

200 g (7 oz/⅔ cup) kewpie mayonnaise (see Note on page 84)

2 tablespoons sriracha or other hot sauce

1 tablespoon extra virgin olive oil

2 spring (green) onions, finely sliced

1 green chilli, deseeded and finely chopped

2 tablespoons finely chopped ginger

1 teaspoon ground cumin

¾ teaspoon ground coriander

2 large free-range eggs, lightly beaten

35 g (1¼ oz/¼ cup) plain (all-purpose) flour

vegetable oil, for deep-frying

Preheat the oven to 180°C/350°F (fan-forced). Line a baking tray with baking paper.

Cut the spaghetti squash in half lengthways and using a spoon, scrape out and discard all the seeds.

Place the squash halves, cut side down, onto the tray. Bake for 30 minutes, or until a skewer passes through the squash easily. Remove from the oven and allow to cool.

Using a fork, tease out the squash flesh to create the spaghetti strands, then transfer to a large mixing bowl.

In a small bowl, combine the mayonnaise and sriracha, mixing thoroughly with a spoon. Set aside.

Heat the olive oil in a small frying pan over medium heat. Add the spring onion, chilli and ginger and sauté for 5 minutes, or until soft. Stir in the cumin and coriander and cook for a further 1 minute.

Add the mixture to the squash, along with the eggs and flour. Season with salt and freshly ground black pepper and gently mix together using a spoon.

Pour 3 cm (1¼ in) of vegetable oil into a medium-sized, heavy-based frying pan. Heat over medium heat until a cooking thermometer registers 180°C (350°F), or until a cube of bread dropped into the oil turns golden brown in 15 seconds.

Heap two tablespoons of the mixture into your hand, then carefully lower into the oil using a slotted spoon. Repeat until the pan is full, but not overcrowded; you will need to cook the patties in several batches.

Cook for about 4 minutes, or until golden brown, turning the patties over halfway through cooking. Using a slotted spoon, transfer the patties to drain briefly on paper towel.

Serve warm, with the sriracha mayonnaise.

BEST IN: AUTUMN & WINTER

Miso ginger baby squash with sesame cucumber salad

SERVES 4

Baby squash can generally be found in greengrocers or supermarkets. Their unique shape and beautiful yellow skin make for a beautiful and tasty dish. –VV

olive oil cooking spray

400 g (14 oz) baby (pattypan) squash, very thinly sliced

MISO GINGER MARINADE

2 tablespoons white miso paste (shiro miso)

1 tablespoon rice vinegar

1½ tablespoons grated palm sugar

1 teaspoon grated ginger

SESAME CUCUMBER SALAD

1 long (telegraph) cucumber, peeled

100 g (3½ oz) bean sprouts

2 spring (green) onions, finely sliced on the diagonal

1 tablespoon sesame seeds

1 tablespoon sesame oil

Preheat the oven to 180°C/350°F (fan-forced). Lightly spray two large baking trays with olive oil spray.

In a medium-sized bowl, whisk together the miso ginger marinade ingredients, along with 1 tablespoon water. Add the squash slices and, using a spoon, gently toss to coat well.

Spread the squash on the baking trays in a single layer. Bake for 10 minutes, then turn the slices over and bake for a further 5 minutes, or until browned.

Meanwhile, in a large mixing bowl, gently toss together the sesame cucumber salad ingredients.

Arrange the salad on a platter, top with the baked squash slices and serve.

BEST IN: SPRING & SUMMER

ALREADY VEGAN!

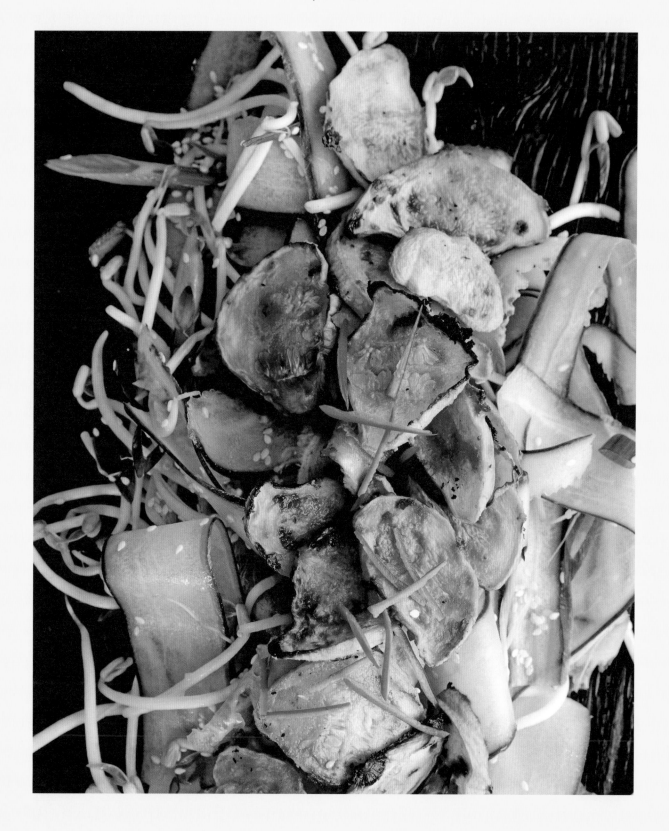

Moroccan pumpkin, sweet potato & lentil soup

SERVES 4

This is a thick and hearty soup, great for a wintery day. Make more than you need, so you can freeze the leftovers for a quick, warming meal another time. The pumpkin breaks down in this soup, while the sweet potato tends to hold its shape more, giving it a satisfying textural contrast.

Ras el hanout is a Moroccan spice blend available from good supermarkets or specialty food stores. –CG

1 tablespoon olive oil

1 onion, chopped

3 garlic cloves, crushed

1.5 kg (3 lb 5 oz) jap or kent pumpkin (winter squash), peeled and cut into 3 cm (1¼ in) chunks

1 sweet potato, peeled and cut into 1.5 cm (½ in) chunks

200 g (7 oz/1 cup) dried red lentils, rinsed

1 teaspoon ras el hanout

1 litre (4 cups) Vegetable stock (see page 23)

TO SERVE

plain yoghurt

handful of coriander (cilantro) leaves

ground sumac

Quick flatbreads (see page 108) or crusty bread

Heat the olive oil in a large heavy-based saucepan over low–medium heat. Sauté the onion and garlic for 6–8 minutes, stirring occasionally, until softened.

Increase the heat to medium and add the pumpkin, sweet potato, lentils and ras el hanout. Cook, stirring occasionally, for 3 minutes, or until the vegetables start to take on a bit of colour.

Pour in the stock, then bring to the boil. Reduce the heat, cover and simmer for 15–20 minutes, stirring occasionally, until the vegetables and lentils are tender. Add a little water to adjust the consistency of the soup if necessary.

Serve the soup thick and chunky, or blend for a smooth soup if you prefer. Serve topped with yoghurt, coriander and a sprinkling of sumac, with flatbreads or crusty bread alongside.

BEST IN: AUTUMN & WINTER

MAKE IT VEGAN!
Serve topped with vegan sour cream or coconut yoghurt.

Indian pumpkin pickle

MAKES 2 × 500 ML (2 CUP) JARS

Eat this pickle as you wish – on rice, with poppadoms, chapatis or alongside any Indian dish. It is a perfect accompaniment to the Biryani-stuffed pumpkins on page 134. –VV

2 tablespoons vegetable oil

1½ teaspoons yellow mustard seeds

2 teaspoons fenugreek seeds

2 red onions, finely sliced

2 garlic cloves, roughly chopped

2 tablespoons finely chopped ginger

2 shallots, finely chopped

4 fresh curry leaves

1 green chilli, deseeded and sliced

2 tablespoons ground coriander

1 tablespoon ground cumin

1 tablespoon ground turmeric

400 g (14 oz) tin chopped tomatoes

60 ml (¼ cup) lime juice

300 ml (10 fl oz) white vinegar

2 teaspoons sea salt

300 g (10½ oz) brown sugar

500 g (1 lb 2 oz) jap or kent pumpkin (winter squash), deseeded and cut into 2 cm (¾ in) cubes

Preheat the oven to 180°C/350°F (fan-forced). Wash two 500 ml (2 cup) jars and lids well with warm soapy water, rinse well and place in the oven for 30 minutes to sterilise. Remove from the oven and set aside until cool enough to handle.

Meanwhile, place a large heavy-based saucepan over medium heat and add the vegetable oil. Once smoking, add the mustard and fenugreek seeds and stir for 1 minute. Add the onion, garlic, ginger, shallot and curry leaves and cook, stirring, for 5 minutes, or until the mixture has browned.

Stir in the green chilli, coriander, cumin and turmeric. Add the tomatoes, lime juice, vinegar, salt and sugar, stirring well.

Add the pumpkin and bring to the boil, then reduce the heat to a simmer. Cover and cook for 15 minutes, or until the pumpkin is just tender.

Allow the mixture to cool slightly, then spoon into the sterilised jars.

Seal and label the jars, then store in a cool, dark place for at least 2 weeks before eating.

Unopened, the jars will keep in the pantry for up to 6 months. Refrigerate after opening and use within 3 weeks.

BEST IN: AUTUMN & WINTER

ALREADY VEGAN!

Biryani-stuffed pumpkins

SERVES 4

These stuffed pumpkins are delightful served as a main meal, or in the centre of the table alongside a curry or stir-fry. –VV

large pinch of saffron threads

4 × 1 kg (2 lb 3 oz) baby kabocha pumpkins (squash), golden nugget pumpkins (minikin squash), or small jap or kent pumpkins (winter squash)

175 g (6 oz/¾ cup) Greek yogurt

450 g (1 lb/2¼ cups) white basmati rice

90 g (3 oz) unsalted butter

GINGER-SPICED PISTACHIOS

90 g (3 oz) unsalted butter

3 brown onions, finely chopped

4 garlic cloves, crushed

80 g (2¾ oz/½ cup) finely chopped fresh ginger

1 green chilli, deseeded and finely chopped

35 g (1¼ oz/¼ cup) pistachios, roughly chopped

30 g (1 oz/¼ cup) dried cranberries, roughly chopped

2 bay leaves

3 small cinnamon sticks

¾ teaspoon chilli powder

1 teaspoon ground cardamom

½ teaspoon grated nutmeg

1 teaspoon ground cloves

2 teaspoons garam masala

Preheat the oven to 180°C/350°F (fan-forced).

Place the saffron threads in a small bowl, pour in 60 ml (¼ cup) warm water and allow to steep until required.

To prepare the ginger-spiced pistachios, place the butter in a saucepan over medium heat. Add the onion and sauté for 10 minutes, or until soft and translucent. Add the garlic and ginger and fry for a further 2 minutes. Stir in the green chilli, pistachios, cranberries and bay leaves. Stir in the remaining spices and turn off the heat. Set aside.

Using a large sharp knife, cut the tops off the pumpkins and set aside. Scrape out the seeds, then place the pumpkin shells on a baking tray. Spoon the spiced pistachio mixture into the pumpkins. Put the lids back on and cover the baking tray with foil.

Bake for about 1 hour, or until a skewer pierces the flesh with ease. Remove from the oven and allow to cool slightly.

Scoop the spiced nut filling and most of the pumpkin flesh out into a saucepan. Stir in the yoghurt and set aside.

Fill a medium-sized saucepan three-quarters full of water and bring to the boil over high heat. Add the rice and cook for 5 minutes, then drain in a colander.

Gently reheat the pumpkin mixture. Working in layers with the rice, fill the pumpkins until full, finishing with a layer of rice. Top the rice with knobs of the butter and drizzle with the saffron water.

Place the lids back on top and cover the baking tray with foil again. Bake for a further 45–60 minutes, until the rice is tender.

Remove the foil and serve immediately.

BEST IN: AUTUMN & WINTER

Pumpkin crisps with honey-spiced macadamias

SERVES 4

These crunchy, earthy crisps can also be enjoyed on their own as a snack, as can the macadamias. They can each be made ahead of time, and stored in separate airtight containers in the pantry for up to a week. –VV

vegetable oil, for deep-frying

1 kg (2 lb 3 oz) jap or kent pumpkin (winter squash), peeled and deseeded

10 sage leaves

HONEY-SPICED MACADAMIAS

2 tablespoons olive oil

1½ tablespoons honey

1 tablespoon smoked paprika

1 garlic clove, crushed

¼ teaspoon chilli powder

1 teaspoon ground cumin

1 teaspoon sea salt

240 g (8½ oz/1½ cups) unsalted macadamia nuts

GARLIC YOGHURT DRESSING

125 g (4½ oz/½ cup) plain yoghurt

¼ teaspoon sea salt

1 tablespoon extra virgin olive oil

1 small garlic clove, peeled and finely grated

Preheat the oven to 180°C/350°F (fan-forced). Line a baking tray with baking paper.

Start by preparing the honey-spiced macadamias. In a small frying pan, combine the olive oil, honey, paprika, garlic, chilli powder, cumin and salt. Stir over low heat for 2–3 minutes, or until melted together and combined.

Turn off the heat and add the macadamias, stirring with a spoon until well coated. Transfer to the baking tray and bake for 10 minutes, turning the nuts over halfway through. Remove from the oven and allow to cool completely.

Put the dressing ingredients in a small bowl and whisk until combined. Set aside.

Pour 6–7 cm (2½–2¾ in) of vegetable oil into a medium-sized heavy-based saucepan. Heat over medium heat until a cooking thermometer registers 160°C (320°F).

Meanwhile, thinly slice the pumpkin using a vegetable peeler, or a mandoline set to its thinnest setting.

Using a slotted spoon, and working in batches, gently lower the pumpkin slices into the oil. Fry for 3–4 minutes, until crisp. Drain on paper towel and repeat until finished.

Add the sage leaves to the oil for 30 seconds, or until crisp, then drain on paper towel.

Arrange the fried pumpkin slices on a serving platter and drizzle with the dressing. Scatter the macadamias and sage over and serve immediately.

BEST IN: AUTUMN & WINTER

Spicy pumpkin dhal

SERVES 4

Warm and spicy dhal is an essential comfort food for the cooler months. It makes a nutritious meal on its own, or is great as a side dish as part of a shared table. –CG

200 g (7 oz/1 cup) split dried mung beans

1 tablespoon peanut oil

1 onion, finely chopped

2 garlic cloves, crushed

1 teaspoon finely grated ginger

1 teaspoon ground coriander

½ teaspoon ground turmeric

750 g (1 lb 11 oz) kent or butternut pumpkin (winter squash), peeled and cut into 2 cm (¾ in) chunks

750 ml (3 cups) Vegetable stock (see page 23)

100 g (3½ oz) baby spinach leaves

handful of fresh coriander (cilantro), roughly chopped, plus extra to garnish

80 ml (⅓ cup) coconut milk

steamed rice or roti, to serve

TEMPER TOPPING

2 tablespoons peanut oil

1 teaspoon black mustard seeds

½ teaspoon cumin seeds

1 small onion, finely sliced

small handful of fresh curry leaves

1 long red chilli, finely sliced

1 tomato, chopped

BEST IN: AUTUMN & WINTER

Rinse the mung beans well, then leave to soak in a large bowl of water overnight.

The next day, drain the mung beans and set aside. Heat the peanut oil in a large saucepan over low–medium heat. Add the onion and cook, stirring occasionally, for 5 minutes, or until soft. Add the garlic, ginger, ground coriander and turmeric and cook, stirring, for 1 minute, or until fragrant.

Add the mung beans and pumpkin. Stir in the stock and bring to the boil over high heat, then reduce the heat to low. Simmer, partially covered, for 30–35 minutes, stirring often, until the pumpkin is breaking down and the mung beans are soft, adding a little water if the mixture is starting to stick. Stir in the spinach, fresh coriander and coconut milk.

For the temper topping, heat the peanut oil in a heavy-based saucepan over medium heat and add the mustard seeds. After a minute or two, when they start to pop, stir in the cumin seeds. Cook for a further 30 seconds, then add the onion, curry leaves and chilli. Cook, stirring, for 2–3 minutes, or until slightly softened. Stir in the tomato and cook for a further 2 minutes, or until the tomato just softens. Transfer to a bowl and set aside until ready to serve.

To serve, ladle the dhal into bowls, spoon the temper topping over the top and garnish with extra coriander. Serve immediately, with rice or roti.

ALREADY VEGAN!

Red curry pumpkin dip

SERVES 4–6

The red curry paste adds a gentle heat to this dip – add a little more for an extra fiery hit. Any leftovers make a great sandwich spread for the following day or two. –CG

2 teaspoons peanut oil

3 red Asian shallots, chopped

2 teaspoons Thai red curry paste

250 g (9 oz) kent or butternut pumpkin (winter squash), peeled and cut into 1 cm (½ in) chunks

2 tablespoons dried red lentils, rinsed

180 ml (¾ cup) Vegetable stock (see page 23)

2 tablespoons coconut cream, plus extra to serve

1 tablespoon lime juice

1 teaspoon coconut sugar

splash of light soy or vegan fish sauce, to taste

handful of fresh coriander (cilantro), chopped

2 tablespoons pumpkin seeds, roughly chopped

roti or vegetable sticks, to serve

BEST IN: AUTUMN & WINTER

Heat the peanut oil in a small heavy-based saucepan over low–medium heat. Stir in the shallot and curry paste. Cover and cook, stirring occasionally, for 5–6 minutes, until soft.

Add the pumpkin, lentils and stock and bring to the boil. Reduce the heat and simmer, uncovered, stirring occasionally, for 15–20 minutes, until the pumpkin and lentils are soft and form a purée. Mash the pumpkin with a spoon as it softens. If the mixture starts sticking to the base of the pan, stir in a little water, though the mixture should be quite thick.

Stir in the coconut cream, lime juice, coconut sugar and soy or fish sauce. Transfer to a serving bowl and set aside to cool. The mixture will thicken slightly on cooling.

Swirl in the coriander and some extra coconut cream. Sprinkle with the pumpkin seeds and serve with flatbreads, roti or vegetable sticks.

Any leftover dip will keep in an airtight container in the fridge for 2–3 days.

ALREADY VEGAN!

Brassicas

broccoli
broccolini
brussels sprouts
cabbage
cauliflower
kale
kohlrabi
wombok

Roasted broccolini, kale & chickpeas with herbed ricotta

SERVES 4

The beauty of this dish lies in the grilling – don't be afraid to char the broccoli a little, as it delivers a great flavour. You can serve this as an individual starter, or as a main with grilled ciabatta. –VV

350 g (12½ oz/2 bunches) broccolini, stems cut in half lengthways

400 g (14 oz) tin chickpeas

1 garlic clove, crushed

60 ml (¼ cup) olive oil, plus extra for drizzling

1 bunch Tuscan kale (cavolo nero), about 550–600 g (1 lb 3–1 lb 5 oz), cut into 2.5 cm (1 in) pieces

250 g (9 oz/1 cup) smooth ricotta

2 tablespoons finely chopped dill

2 tablespoons finely chopped basil

1 teaspoon grated lemon zest

1 tablespoon lemon juice

pinch of chilli flakes

MAKE IT VEGAN!
Substitute the ricotta with a soft vegan cheese, or leave it out altogether and serve the salad on top of some hummus.

Preheat the oven to 180°C/350°F (fan-forced). Preheat the grill (broiler) to medium.

In a mixing bowl, toss the broccolini, chickpeas and garlic with 2 tablespoons of the olive oil. Spread the mixture onto a baking tray.

In another bowl, toss the kale with the remaining olive oil, then spread over another two baking trays.

Place the broccolini mixture under the grill and cook for 4–5 minutes, then turn the broccolini over and cook for a further 4–5 minutes, until nicely chargrilled. Remove from the heat and set aside to cool.

Meanwhile, transfer the kale trays to the oven and bake for 3–4 minutes, or until starting to brown, then turn the kale over and bake for a further 2 minutes, or until crisp. Remove from the oven and set aside to cool.

In a small bowl, combine the ricotta, dill, basil, lemon zest, lemon juice and chilli flakes. Season with salt and mix together with a spoon.

Smear the ricotta mixture onto a serving plate and top with the kale and broccolini mixture.

Drizzle with a little extra olive oil and serve.

BEST IN: AUTUMN, WINTER & SPRING

Orzo salad with kale, broccoli & lemon

SERVES 4–6

Also known as risoni, orzo is a type of pasta shaped like a large grain of rice. Its small shape makes it quick for cooking, and ideal for adding to a wide variety of dishes such as soups and casseroles. Here, it features in a light, lemony salad that is lovely served warm as a main meal, or the next day cold. Preserved lemon rind really brings a lot of flavour to this dish – if you're a fan, you can always add more. –VV

350 g (12½ oz) head of broccoli, cut into florets

330 g (11½ oz/1½ cups) orzo

4–5 kale leaves, roughly chopped

3 garlic cloves, crushed

80 g (2¾ oz/1 cup) grated parmesan

1 tablespoon grated lemon zest

60 ml (¼ cup) lemon juice

80 ml (⅓ cup) extra virgin olive oil

125 g (4½ oz/½ cup) sour cream

1 teaspoon finely chopped red chilli

150 g (5½ oz/1 cup) pine nuts, toasted

2 tablespoons finely sliced preserved lemon rind, or the shredded zest of 1 lemon

Fill a large saucepan with water and place over high heat. Bring to the boil and add the broccoli florets. Blanch for 2 minutes, then remove with a slotted spoon and refresh under cold running water. Set aside.

Add the orzo to the boiling water and cook for 4–6 minutes, until tender. Strain in a fine-mesh sieve and rinse under cold water to cool. Set aside to drain.

Place about 1 cup of the broccoli in a food processor. Add the kale, garlic, parmesan, lemon zest, lemon juice, olive oil, sour cream, chilli and half the pine nuts. Pulse until smooth, then season with salt and freshly ground black pepper.

In a large bowl, mix together the orzo and remaining broccoli. Fold the kale mixture through.

Top with the remaining pine nuts, garnish with the perserved lemon rind or lemon zest and serve.

BEST IN: AUTUMN, WINTER & SPRING

Broccolini with poached eggs & miso hollandaise

SERVES 4

Furikake is a Japanese seasoning, typically made with seaweed, sesame seeds and salt, often used to sprinkle over rice dishes. You'll find it in Japanese grocery stores and Asian food markets. –CG

4 very fresh free-range eggs

a dash of vinegar

350 g (12½ oz/2 bunches) broccolini, trimmed

furikake seasoning, for sprinkling

MISO HOLLANDAISE

60 g (2 oz) butter, softened

2 teaspoons white miso paste (shiro miso)

2 free-range egg yolks

1 tablespoon rice wine vinegar

freshly ground white pepper, to taste

For the hollandaise, stir the butter and miso paste together in a small bowl until combined. Set aside.

Bring a medium-sized saucepan of water to a simmer over low heat. Whisk the egg yolks and rice wine vinegar in a medium-sized heatproof bowl until combined, then place over the pan of simmering water; the bowl should fit snugly on top of the saucepan and should not touch the water.

Whisk for 2–3 minutes, or until the mixture becomes thick and pale. Add the miso butter mixture, a teaspoon at a time, whisking until combined before adding the next – this may take 6–8 minutes. Remove from the heat and season to taste with white pepper.

Sit the hollandaise in a warm spot, covered, whisking occasionally until ready to serve. It should hold for about 30 minutes or so. Just before serving, you can thin the hollandaise out by whisking in a little warm water if required.

To poach the eggs, two-thirds fill a small saucepan with water and bring to a very gentle simmer. Add the vinegar. Crack an egg into a small bowl. Using spoon, make a whirlpool in the simmering water and gently slide the egg in. Simmer very gently for 3–4 minutes, or until the white is set. Remove with a slotted spoon, transfer to a plate and cover with foil to keep warm. Poach the remaining eggs in the same way.

While the final egg is poaching, steam the broccolini in a large covered steamer basket set over a saucepan of boiling water for 3–4 minutes, until tender.

Serve the broccolini immediately, topped with a drizzle of hollandaise, the poached eggs and a sprinkling of furikake seasoning.

BEST IN: AUTUMN, WINTER & SPRING

Roast cauliflower with pomegranate & yoghurt

SERVES 4

Cauliflower is such an undervalued vegetable. Here is a great way to make the most of this beautiful brassica. To really bring flavour to the table, use a good-quality curry powder. –VV

olive oil cooking spray

1.5 kg (3 lb 5 oz) head of cauliflower, cut into florets

1 teaspoon Indian-style curry powder

1 teaspoon ground cumin

1 teaspoon sea salt

90 ml (⅓ cup) olive oil

1 short cucumber

180 g (6½ oz/⅔ cup) Greek-style yoghurt

large handful of coriander (cilantro), roughly chopped, plus extra leaves to garnish

large handful of mint, roughly chopped

2 spring (green) onions, finely sliced

40 g (1½ oz/⅓ cup) flaked almonds, toasted

seeds of 1 small pomegranate (see Note on page 66)

Preheat the oven to 180°C/350°F (fan-forced). Spray a baking tray with olive oil.

Place the cauliflower, curry powder, cumin, salt and 60 ml (¼ cup) of the olive oil in a mixing bowl and toss to coat. Spread the mixture over the baking tray and roast for 20 minutes, or until the cauliflower florets are tender.

Remove from the oven and allow to cool completely.

Meanwhile, grate the cucumber, leaving the skin on if you wish. Squeeze out the excess liquid and place the cucumber in a small bowl. Stir the remaining olive oil and yoghurt through, season to taste with salt and freshly ground black pepper, then set aside.

Transfer the roasted cauliflower to a mixing bowl. Add the coriander, mint, spring onion, almonds and pomegranate seeds. Toss together and transfer to a serving plate.

Top with lashings of the yoghurt mixture, garnish with extra coriander and serve.

BEST IN: AUTUMN, WINTER & SPRING

MAKE IT VEGAN!
Just replace the yoghurt with your favourite vegan yoghurt.

Cauliflower 'tabbouleh' salad

SERVES 4

This zesty, brightly flavoured dish is great when freshly made, but it's also satisfying eaten over the following day or two and makes a great addition to picnics or lunch boxes. For those cutting down on their carbs, replacing the usual cracked wheat with cauliflower is a tasty alternative. —CG

400 g (14 oz) head of cauliflower, including some stalk

2 tomatoes, chopped

1 cucumber, chopped

2 spring (green) onions, chopped

large handful of mint, roughly chopped

large handful of parsley, roughly chopped

finely grated zest of 1 lemon

2 tablespoons lemon juice

2 tablespoons extra virgin olive oil

2 tablespoons pecans, toasted

ground sumac, for sprinkling

Finely slice the stalk of the cauliflower and cut the remainder into florets.

Bring a large saucepan of water to the boil. Add the cauliflower stalks to a steamer basket, sitting the florets on top. Set the basket over the pan of boiling water, then cover and steam for 4 minutes, or until barely tender. Set aside to cool.

Working in two batches, put the cooled cauliflower in a food processor and pulse until chopped. Do not over-process, as you want the cauliflower to retain a coarse grain-like texture. Transfer to a large bowl.

Add the tomato, cucumber, spring onion and herbs and toss to combine. Stir in the lemon zest, lemon juice and olive oil. Season to taste with salt and freshly ground black pepper.

Serve, scattered with the pecans and sprinkled with a little sumac.

BEST IN: AUTUMN, WINTER & SPRING

ALREADY VEGAN!

Three-way cauliflower soup

SERVES 4

Cooking the cauliflower in three different ways intensifies the flavour of this otherwise 'simple' soup. The longer cooking time brings out its natural sweetness, the less-cooked cauliflower adds a fresh vibrancy, while the roasted cauliflower adds another dimension of sweetness and texture. –CG

2 tablespoons olive oil

4 shallots, chopped

1.2 kg (2 lb 10 oz) head of cauliflower, stalk finely sliced, the remainder cut into 3–4 cm (1½ in) florets

about 1 litre (4 cups) Vegetable stock (see page 23)

1 loaf sourdough bread, torn into large breadcrumbs

sour cream or plain yoghurt, to serve

fresh herbs, to garnish

MAKE IT VEGAN!
Serve with a nice dollop of vegan sour cream or yoghurt.

Heat half the olive oil in a large heavy-based saucepan over low heat. Add the shallot and cook for 6–7 minutes, until tender. Add the cauliflower stalk and just over half of the florets. Cook, stirring, for 2 minutes, then add enough stock to cover. Bring to the boil, reduce the heat and simmer, partially covered, for 30 minutes.

Meanwhile, preheat the oven to 200°C/400°F (fan-forced). Line a baking tray with baking paper.

Put half the remaining cauliflower in a mixing bowl. Add the breadcrumbs and remaining olive oil and toss until coated. Spread the cauliflower florets over the tray, reserving the crumbs at the bottom of the bowl. Roast for 10 minutes, then add the reserved breadcrumbs to the baking tray and roast for a further 5–10 minutes, or until the cauliflower is tender and browned, and the crumbs are crisp.

Add the remaining raw cauliflower to the soup and simmer, uncovered, for 10–12 minutes, until the cauliflower is tender. Remove from the heat and allow to cool slightly.

Blend the soup until smooth and silky. Season with salt and freshly ground black pepper and reheat gently over medium heat.

Serve the soup topped with the roasted cauliflower and crumbs, a dollop of sour cream or yoghurt, and your choice of herbs.

BEST IN: AUTUMN, WINTER & SPRING

Cauliflower 'steaks' with tahini & mint dressing

SERVES 4

You should get at least two very shapely 'steaks' from one cauliflower. That doesn't mean the rest will go to waste – there will still be plenty of flat surface area that will brown beautifully. Add some protein in the form of legumes for a great meal, or serve as a side dish. The roasted cauliflower is also excellent with the salsa verde on page 42. And the dressing is very versatile too – use it to jazz up a simple salad or drizzle over steamed vegetables. –CG

1 small cauliflower, about 1 kg (2 lb 3 oz), stalk left intact

olive oil, for drizzling

2 garlic cloves, unpeeled but lightly bruised

roughly chopped pistachios, to garnish

TAHINI & MINT DRESSING

125 g (4½ oz/½ cup) Greek-style yoghurt

handful of mint leaves, chopped

3 teaspoons unhulled tahini

juice of ½ lemon

1 teaspoon pomegranate molasses

freshly ground white pepper, to taste

MAKE IT VEGAN!
Use vegan yoghurt or soft cream cheese for the dressing.

Preheat the oven to 160°C/320°F (fan-forced). Line a baking tray with baking paper.

Trim off the very bottom of the cauliflower stalk, keeping most of it attached. Place the cauliflower on a cutting board with the stem side down. Cut the cauliflower from the top and down through the stalk, into slices about 1.5 cm (½ in) thick. Drizzle with a little olive oil and rub over the cauliflower.

Heat a large heavy-based frying pan over medium–high heat. Add half the cauliflower (including any pieces that didn't form complete slices) and garlic. Cook the cauliflower for 2 minutes on each side, or until golden. Transfer the cauliflower and garlic to the baking tray.

Cook the remaining cauliflower and garlic in the same way and add to the baking tray. Transfer to the oven and bake for 15–20 minutes, or until the cauliflower is tender.

Meanwhile, for the dressing, whisk the yoghurt, mint, tahini, lemon juice and pomegranate molasses until combined. Season with a little salt and white pepper. Any dressing left over after you've dressed the salad will keep in an airtight container in the fridge for up to 3 days.

When the cauliflower is done, remove the roasted garlic cloves and leave to cool a little, then squeeze out the soft cloves, discarding the skin. Mash the roasted garlic and mix it through the dressing. Add a little cold water if needed to bring the dressing to a pouring consistency.

Serve the cauliflower steaks warm, drizzled with the dressing and scattered with pistachios.

BEST IN: AUTUMN, WINTER & SPRING

Kale, ricotta & feta rolls

SERVES 4 / MAKES 8

These are great straight from the oven, but also well worth eating after a day or two in the fridge. Serve with a baby rocket (arugula) and spinach salad. Or try the Spiced rhubarb chutney (see page 35), Indian-style tomato chutney (see page 97) or a good dollop of your favourite hot sauce. –CG

1 tablespoon olive oil

1 onion, finely chopped

2 garlic cloves, crushed

400 g (14 oz) bunch of Tuscan kale
(cavolo nero), stalks and veins removed,
leaves shredded

200 g (7 oz) fresh firm ricotta, crumbled

100 g (3½ oz) feta, crumbled

2 large free-range eggs, lightly beaten

2 tablespoons fresh wholemeal
(whole-wheat) breadcrumbs

1 teaspoon ground cumin

finely grated zest of 1 lemon

5 sheets filo pastry

olive oil cooking spray

sesame seeds, for sprinkling

ground sumac, for sprinkling

Heat the olive oil in a large heavy-based saucepan over medium heat. Sauté the onion and garlic for 5–6 minutes, or until the onion is tender. Add the kale and cook, stirring occasionally, for 8 minutes, or until wilted and tender. Remove from the heat, transfer to a large bowl and set aside to cool.

Preheat the oven to 200°C/400°F (fan-forced). Line a baking tray with baking paper.

Add the cheeses, beaten egg, breadcrumbs, cumin and lemon zest to the cooled kale mixture. Season with a little salt and freshly ground black pepper and mix well.

Place one sheet of filo on a flat surface. (Cover the remaining filo sheets with a clean damp tea towel, so they don't dry out.)

Spray the filo sheet with a little olive oil and top with another sheet of filo. Repeat the layering with the remaining filo, spraying each sheet with more oil each time.

Cut the layered filo in half widthways, to give two pieces. Spoon half the kale mixture along the side of the filo closest to you, then roll up firmly to enclose the filling. Using a serrated knife, carefully cut the roll into four equal portions. Transfer to the baking tray, placing them seam side down.

Repeat with the remaining filo and filling, to make eight rolls in total. Spray with a little more olive oil and sprinkle with the sesame seeds and sumac.

Bake for 25–30 minutes, or until the pastry is crisp and the filling is cooked through. If making the rolls ahead of time, reheat in a 160°C/320°F (fan-forced) oven for 10–15 minutes until the pastry is crisp and the rolls are heated through.

BEST IN: WINTER & SPRING

Kimchi with turmeric

MAKES 2 × 750 ML (3 CUP) JARS

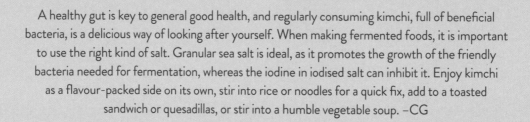

A healthy gut is key to general good health, and regularly consuming kimchi, full of beneficial bacteria, is a delicious way of looking after yourself. When making fermented foods, it is important to use the right kind of salt. Granular sea salt is ideal, as it promotes the growth of the friendly bacteria needed for fermentation, whereas the iodine in iodised salt can inhibit it. Enjoy kimchi as a flavour-packed side on its own, stir into rice or noodles for a quick fix, add to a toasted sandwich or quesadillas, or stir into a humble vegetable soup. –CG

1 large wombok (Chinese cabbage), about 1.3 kg (2 lb 14 oz)

1½ tablespoons granular sea salt

1 tablespoon brown rice flour

1½ tablespoons gochugaru (Korean red pepper flakes), or to taste

1½ tablespoons finely grated fresh turmeric

1 teaspoon finely grated ginger

2 carrots, shredded

1 small daikon, about 400 g (14 oz), peeled and shredded

3 spring (green) onions, cut into 3 cm (1¼ in) lengths

3 small red chillies, sliced

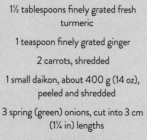

ALREADY VEGAN!

Discard the outer leaves of the cabbage, reserving one leaf to later place in the jars, to keep the shredded cabbage submerged.

Quarter the cabbage and remove the core. Cut the cabbage horizontally into 5 cm (2 in) pieces. Layer them in a very large stainless steel or glass bowl, sprinkling with the salt as you go. Set aside for 10 minutes.

'Massage' the cabbage with your hands, squeezing firmly to help release the liquid from the cabbage, until the volume of the cabbage has reduced by more than half; this will take about 5 minutes. Liquid will be pooling in the bottom of the bowl.

At this point you want the cabbage to be covered with liquid, so add enough water to the bowl to just cover the cabbage, if necessary. Set aside for 1–2 hours, or until the thickest pieces of cabbage are starting to look translucent.

Meanwhile, preheat the oven to 180°C/350°F (fan-forced). Wash two 750 ml (3 cup) jars with warm soapy water, rinse well and place in the oven for 30 minutes to sterilise.

Remove the jars from the oven and leave until cool.

Reserve about 125 ml (½ cup) of the cabbage brine, then drain and rinse the cabbage very well. Set aside to drain while preparing the spice paste.

In a small saucepan, combine the rice flour and 60 ml (¼ cup) water, mixing until smooth. Cook over medium heat, stirring, for 1–2 minutes, until thickened. Remove from the heat and leave to cool, then stir in the gochugaru, turmeric and ginger.

Put the cabbage and spice paste into a large bowl. Add the carrot, daikon, spring onion and chilli. Wearing food-handling gloves, massage the spice paste through the vegetables until they are all thoroughly coated, and the juice starts to run again.

Pack the cabbage mixture into the prepared jars a few handfuls at a time, pressing down firmly each time to exclude air from the mixture, before adding more cabbage mixture. Add all the liquid from the bowl as well; it should cover the cabbage with room to spare.

Cut the reserved cabbage leaf so that it will fit snugly into the jars. Press it over the kimchi mixture to keep it submerged by at least 2 cm (¾ in). Add the reserved brine if necessary. To keep the cabbage submerged under the brine, add stone or glass weights if you have them, or you can use a small jar that will fit through the top filled with water. If the vessel is quite full, keep it on a plate to catch any overflowing liquid.

Loosely cap the jars, or cover with a clean cloth. Place the jars in a cool, dark place (18–22°C/64–72°F is ideal) and leave for 2–5 days. During this time, check the kimchi daily, tasting to see if it is fermented enough for your liking, and pressing the cabbage mixture down if it has floated above the liquid. It is important that the cabbage mixture always remains submerged beneath the liquid. If necessary, top up the jars with a 2 per cent saline solution, made by dissolving 1 teaspoon salt in 300 ml (10½ fl oz) water.

The rate of fermentation will vary, depending on the climate and humidity.

When your kimchi is ready, seal with sterilised lids and keep in the fridge, where it should keep for months.

BEST IN: AUTUMN, WINTER & SPRING

Mixed vegetable pickle

MAKES 1 × 1 LITRE (4 CUP) JAR

Cauliflower is the unassuming hero of this pickle and it really does shine when treated in this way. Pickled vegetables are a great appetiser, perfect for nibbling on when you fancy a healthy snack, or lovely as part of a sharing table to add a pop of brightness to the meal. –CG

60 g (2 oz/¼ cup) table salt

350 g (12½ oz) small cauliflower florets

2 small shallots

5 baby carrots, lightly scrubbed

2 carrots, peeled and sliced

5 cherry tomatoes

3 small jalapeño chillies

1 teaspoon coriander seeds

1 teaspoon yellow mustard seeds

PICKLING VINEGAR

1 tablespoon coriander seeds

1 tablespoon yellow mustard seeds

2 teaspoons whole cloves

1 teaspoon black peppercorns

1 teaspoon allspice berries

1 cinnamon stick

2 dried bay leaves

750 ml (3 cups) apple cider vinegar

Put the salt in a large glass or stainless steel bowl, add 750 ml (3 cups) water and stir to dissolve. Add the cauliflower, shallot, carrots, tomatoes and chillies, mixing to combine. Cover the bowl and leave to stand overnight.

Meanwhile, make the pickling vinegar. Bruise all the spices gently using a mortar and pestle. Place the spices in a stainless steel saucepan and pour in the vinegar. Heat gently until the mixture comes to the boil, then remove from the heat. Leave to cool for at least 2 hours, or overnight if possible.

When you are ready to continue, preheat the oven to 180°C/350°F (fan-forced). Wash a 1 litre (4 cup) jar and lid with warm soapy water, rinse well and place in the oven for 30 minutes to sterilise them.

Remove the jar and lid from the oven and set aside until cool enough to handle.

Strain the pickling vinegar through a triple thickness of muslin (cheesecloth), into a jug or bowl. Discard the spices.

Rinse the vegetables under cold water, drain, then dry with paper towel.

Add the coriander and mustard seeds to the sterilised jar, then pack with the dried vegetables. Pour in the strained vinegar until the vegetables are completely covered.

Seal and label the jar and keep at room temperature for 2 days, before moving to the refrigerator. Leave for at least 1 week before eating. The pickle will keep in the fridge for up to 3 months.

BEST IN: AUTUMN, WINTER & SPRING

ALREADY VEGAN!

Okonomiyaki

SERVES 4

Making okonomiyaki is a great way to use up some of those neglected veggies at the back of the fridge. Once you have your cabbage base, add a good handful or two of chopped green beans, peas, broad (fava) beans, broccoli, cauliflower or steamed diced sweet potato to replace the edamame and corn. Okonomi sauce, the umami-packed condiment generously squeezed over the top of the okonomiyaki, is available from Asian grocery stores or the international aisle in supermarkets. –CG

150 g (5½ oz/1 cup) frozen podded edamame (young green soy beans)

1 tablespoon peanut oil, plus extra for pan-frying

1 red onion, sliced

2 garlic cloves, crushed

150 g (5½ oz) red cabbage, shredded

150 g (5½ oz) white cabbage, shredded

kernels from 1 fresh corn cob

4 spring (green) onions, thinly sliced

100 g (3½ oz/⅔ cup) plain (all-purpose) flour

3 teaspoons baking powder

4 large free-range eggs

1 teaspoon white miso paste (shiro miso)

1 tablespoon sesame seeds

kewpie mayonnaise (see Note on page 84), to serve

okonomi sauce, to serve

micro herbs or extra sliced spring (green) onion, to garnish

Fill a small saucepan with water and bring to the boil over high heat. Add the frozen edamame and return to the boil. Drain in a colander, refresh under cold water until cooled, then drain well and set aside.

Heat the peanut oil in a heavy-based frying pan over medium heat. Sauté the onion and garlic, stirring occasionally, for 4–5 minutes, until softened.

Transfer the mixture to a large bowl and set aside to cool. Add the edamame, cabbage, corn and spring onion and mix well. Sift the flour and baking powder over the top, then mix well to coat all the vegetables in the flour.

In a bowl, whisk together the eggs and miso until combined. Add to the vegetable mixture and mix through well.

Heat the same frying pan over low–medium heat. Preheat the oven to 100°C/210°F (fan-forced). Line a baking tray with baking paper.

Add a little more peanut oil to the pan, then spoon one-quarter of the mixture into the pan. Spread gently to make one large pancake about 1.5 cm (½ in) thick. Cook for 4–5 minutes on each side, or until a golden crust has formed and the pancake is cooked through. Transfer to the baking tray, cover loosely with foil and keep warm in the oven.

Cook another three pancakes in the same way, transferring each batch to the oven to keep warm; if you have two frying pans, try cooking two pancakes at once to speed things up.

Serve the okonomiyaki warm, drizzled with mayonnaise and okonomi sauce, and garnished with micro herbs or spring onion.

BEST IN: AUTUMN & SPRING

Shaved brussels sprouts & freekeh salad

SERVES 4

Brussels sprouts are truly delicious when given a chance to shine. In this recipe they are shaved super-fine and eaten as a salad ingredient, deliciously paired with a sprightly dressing and refreshing herbs. Freekeh is a highly nutritious grain made from roasted green grains (usually wheat). It has a lovely chewiness that adds another dimension to this salad.–CG

90 g (3 oz/½ cup) cracked freekeh

200 g (7 oz) brussels sprouts, trimmed

3 spring (green) onions, finely sliced

handful of mint, roughly chopped

handful of coriander (cilantro) leaves

handful of pomegranate seeds

2 tablespoons walnuts, toasted and roughly chopped (optional)

ORANGE & POMEGRANATE DRESSING

60 ml (¼ cup) orange juice

2 tablespoons olive oil

1 tablespoon sherry vinegar

1 teaspoon pomegranate molasses

1 teaspoon vegan dijon mustard

1 small garlic clove, crushed

Cook the freekeh in a large saucepan of lightly salted boiling water for 15–20 minutes, or until al dente. Rinse under cold running water, then drain well, squeezing out as much water as possible.

Meanwhile, for the dressing, combine the ingredients in a jar. Seal with the lid and shake until well combined. Season to taste.

Using a sharp knife, or a mandoline if you have one, shave the brussels sprouts lengthways as finely as you can.

Put the cooled freekeh in a large bowl. Add the shaved sprouts, spring onion and herbs, and toss to combine. Drizzle with the dressing and toss until mixed through.

Serve sprinkled with the pomegranate seeds, and walnuts if using.

BEST IN: AUTUMN & WINTER

ALREADY VEGAN!

Raw kohlrabi & cabbage salad with peanut, lime & sesame dressing

SERVES 4

Using a black sesame cracker for a base makes a beautiful textural addition to this fragrant salad. You'll find these in Asian grocery stores, but if you can't find one, simply dish up the salad on a plate or in a bowl.

This salad is best made just before serving. –VV

1 large Vietnamese black sesame cracker, to serve

crushed peanuts, to garnish

crispy fried shallots, to garnish

coriander (cilantro), to garnish

KOHLRABI & CABBAGE SALAD

2 purple kohlrabi, about 500 g (1 lb 2 oz) in total, cut into thin strips

2 carrots, cut into thin strips

¼ small cabbage, finely shredded

2 spring (green) onions, finely sliced

handful of Vietnamese mint, finely chopped

90 g (3 oz/1 cup) bean sprouts

1 small red onion, finely chopped

1 red chilli, finely chopped

PEANUT, LIME & SESAME DRESSING

1 tablespoon rice vinegar

1½ tablespoons light soy sauce

3 tablespoons crunchy peanut butter

1 tablespoon lime juice

1 tablespoon sesame oil

Combine all the kohlrabi salad ingredients in a large bowl. Set aside.

Prepare the black sesame cracker according to the packet instructions.

In a small bowl, whisk together all the dressing ingredients. Pour the dressing over the salad and toss to coat thoroughly.

Transfer the salad onto the sesame cracker. Garnish with crushed peanuts, fried shallots and coriander and serve straight away, inviting diners to break off chunks from the cracker and help themselves.

BEST IN: AUTUMN, WINTER & SPRING

ALREADY VEGAN!

Cabbage rolls stuffed with black rice & raisins

MAKES 20

You'll find cabbage rolls all across Europe, each country having its own version. The addition of black rice and raisins is a nod to the dish's Middle Eastern counterpart, known as dolmathes or dolmades. –VV

26 cabbage leaves

140 ml (4½ fl oz) olive oil

155 g (5½ oz/1 cup) pine nuts

3 large brown onions, finely chopped

140 g (5 oz/⅔ cup) short-grain white rice

65 g (2¼ oz/⅓ cup) long-grain black rice

2 teaspoons sea salt

½ teaspoon freshly ground black pepper

1 teaspoon ground allspice

small handful of dill leaves, chopped

small handful of mint leaves, chopped

small handful of parsley, chopped

30 g (1 oz/¼ cup) raisins

30 g (1 oz/¼ cup) slivered almonds

125 g (4½ oz/½ cup) tomato paste (concentrated purée)

ALREADY VEGAN!

Bring a large saucepan of water to a simmer over medium heat. Add the cabbage leaves, in batches if necessary, and blanch for 5–6 minutes, until pliable. Gently drain in a colander, then use a sharp knife to trim away and discard any thick centre ribs on the leaves. Set aside to cool.

Place a medium-sized saucepan over high heat. Pour in 60 ml (¼ cup) of the olive oil and pine nuts and stir for 1 minute, or until golden brown. Reduce the heat to medium, then add the onion and sauté for 15 minutes, or until softened.

Stir in both the white and black rice and cook for a further 3 minutes. Add the salt, pepper, allspice and 500 ml (2 cups) warm water. Bring to the boil, then reduce the heat to low. Cover and cook for 15 minutes, or until the water has been absorbed and the rice is just cooked.

Remove from the heat, then stir in the dill, mint, parsley, raisins and almonds. Put the lid back on and set aside to cool to room temperature.

In a large saucepan, warm the remaining olive oil over medium heat. Add the tomato paste and 500 ml (2 cups) water. Whisk until smooth, then set aside.

Place six cabbage leaves on the base of a large heavy-based saucepan, with the tomato stock. Use the remaining cabbage leaves for your rolls. Lay a few cabbage leaves on a clean work surface and spoon 2 heaped teaspoons of the rice mixture onto the middle of each leaf. Fold in the sides, then roll the cabbage leaf up tight. Place seam side down into the tomato stock, packing them in nice and tight. Repeat with the remaining cabbage leaves and filling, packing the rolls tightly in the pan. Sit a heatproof plate directly on top of the rolls, then put the lid on.

Bring to a simmer over low–medium heat and cook for 45 minutes. Using tongs, carefully remove the rolls. Inspect the liquid in the pan – if it is too watery, continue simmering for a further 10–15 minutes. Serve the rolls on a serving platter, drizzled with some of the pan juices.

BEST IN: AUTUMN, WINTER & SPRING

Roasted maple sprouts with pecans

SERVES 4

The humble brussels sprout is an often loathed member of the brassica family — unfairly so! Roasting really brings out their beautiful nutty flavour. Sweetened with maple syrup, and topped with crunchy pecans, this knockout dish will charm even the haters. –VV

75 g (2¾ oz/¾ cup) pecans

600 g (1 lb 5 oz) brussels sprouts, trimmed and halved

1 fuji apple, cored and sliced into eighths

2 tablespoons olive oil, plus extra for greasing

2½ tablespoons balsamic vinegar

3 tablespoons maple syrup

ALREADY VEGAN!

Preheat the oven to 180°C/350°F (fan-forced).

Spread the pecans on a baking tray and bake for 3–4 minutes, until lightly toasted. Remove from the oven and allow to cool, then roughly chop and set aside.

Increase the oven temperature to 200°C/400°F (fan-forced). Lightly oil a baking tray.

In a mixing bowl, toss the brussels sprouts and apple slices with the olive oil. Transfer to the baking tray and roast for 20 minutes, turning once.

Remove from the oven and place the mixture in a large serving bowl. Drizzle with the balsamic vinegar and maple syrup, tossing gently to coat.

Serve immediately, topped with the chopped pecans.

BEST IN: AUTUMN & WINTER

Roots

beetroot

carrots

celeriac

daikon

lotus root

parsnips

radishes

turnips

Roasted parsnips with hazelnuts & feta

SERVES 4

If you can't find baby parsnips, larger parsnips cut lengthways into quarters will do the trick. The nuttiness of parsnips and hazelnuts pair very well together. –CG

600 g (1 lb 5 oz) baby parsnips, trimmed and scrubbed, or regular parsnips, cut lengthways into quarters

8 garlic cloves, unpeeled, lightly bruised

1 tablespoon olive oil

2 tablespoons hazelnuts, roughly chopped

1 tablespoon verjuice or lemon juice

80 g (2¾ oz) marinated soft feta

Preheat the oven to 200°C/400°F (fan-forced). Line a roasting tin with baking paper.

Spread the parsnips and garlic cloves in the roasting tin. Drizzle with the olive oil, toss to coat, then spread out in a single layer.

Bake for 20 minutes, then turn the parsnips over and scatter with the chopped hazelnuts. Return to the oven and roast for a further 10 minutes, or until the parsnips are tender and browned.

Serve immediately, drizzled with the verjuice or lemon juice and scattered with the feta.

BEST IN: AUTUMN & WINTER

MAKE IT VEGAN!
Use a soft vegan cheese instead of the feta, or add some diced avocado instead.

Roasted carrot soup with coriander & mint pesto

SERVES 4–6

Roasting the carrots concentrates their flavour and brings out their inherent sweetness, highlighted by the Asian-inspired coriander and mint pesto. Enjoy with the Quick flatbreads on page 108, or with roti or chapatis, reheated in a hot frying pan until flaky and crisp. –CG

800 g (1 lb 12 oz) carrots

1 large parsnip

1 large onion, coarsely chopped

1 tablespoon peanut oil

1 tablespoon shaved palm sugar or
2 teaspoons maple syrup

2 teaspoons ground cumin

pinch of chilli flakes

1 litre (4 cups) Vegetable stock
(see page 23)

coriander (cilantro) leaves, to garnish

unsalted roasted peanuts, to serve

roti, to serve

CORIANDER & MINT PESTO

25 g (1 oz/¾ cup) coriander (cilantro) leaves

5 g (¼ oz/¼ cup) mint leaves

1 small garlic clove, crushed

2 tablespoons unsalted roasted peanuts

1 tablespoon lime juice, or to taste

80 ml (⅓ cup) peanut oil

Preheat the oven to 180°C/350°F (fan-forced). Line two baking trays with baking paper.

Trim the carrots and parsnip. Scrub the carrots, then cut them in half lengthways. Peel and quarter the parsnip lengthways.

Spread the carrot, parsnip and onion on the baking trays. Drizzle with the peanut oil and toss to coat, spreading them out in a single layer. Sprinkle with the palm sugar, cumin and chilli flakes, and season with salt and freshly ground black pepper. Roast for 30–35 minutes, or until the vegetables are soft and browned. Set aside to cool slightly.

Meanwhile, for the pesto, whiz the coriander, mint, garlic and peanuts in a food processor or blender until finely chopped. With the motor running, add the lime juice and peanut oil in a thin, steady stream until combined. Transfer to a bowl and season to taste, adding a little more lime juice if necessary. Set aside.

Transfer the roasted vegetables and any sticky baking juices to a food processor or blender and whiz until smooth.

Transfer the mixture to a large heavy-based saucepan and stir in the stock and enough water to bring to the desired consistency. Bring to the boil over medium heat, then reduce the heat slightly and simmer for 5 minutes, or until heated through. Season to taste.

Ladle the soup into bowls. Drizzle with the pesto, scatter with the coriander and peanuts and serve immediately, with roti on the side.

BEST IN: AUTUMN, WINTER & SPRING

ALREADY VEGAN!

Carrot, cauliflower, broccoli & mustard gratin

SERVES 4

Creamy gouda and havarti cheese create a beautiful rich sauce for this classic dish. If you're after a little more 'bite', try adding some parmesan and chilli flakes as well. –VV

3 carrots, sliced into 2.5 cm (1 inch) rounds

250 g (9 oz/2 cups) cauliflower florets

180 g (6½ oz/3 cups) broccoli florets

1 small brown onion, cut into eighths

2 tablespoons arrowroot or tapioca flour

375 ml (1½ cups) full-fat milk

35 g (1¼ oz/¼ cup) grated gouda

75 g (2¾ oz/½ cup) grated havarti

2 teaspoons wholegrain mustard

1 teaspoon chopped fresh rosemary

1 tablespoon olive oil

35 g (1¼ oz/⅓ cup) dry breadcrumbs

Preheat the oven to 180°C/350°F (fan-forced).

Bring a large saucepan of water to the boil and set a large steamer on top. Place the carrot, cauliflower and broccoli in the steamer basket, then cover and steam for 8 minutes, or until the vegetables are just tender. Remove from the steamer and place in a 20 cm × 25 cm (8 in × 10 in) baking dish, along with the onion, ensuring all the vegetables are evenly distributed.

In a small bowl, whisk together the arrowroot powder and 60 ml (¼ cup) cold water, to a smooth slurry.

Pour the milk into a medium-sized saucepan over medium heat, stirring constantly for 4 minutes, or until warm. Add the arrowroot slurry and stir constantly for 1 minute. Add the gouda, havarti, mustard and rosemary and stir until the cheese has melted and the sauce is smooth. Set aside.

In a small frying pan, heat the olive oil over medium heat. Add the breadcrumbs and heat through for 2 minutes, stirring constantly.

Pour the cheesy sauce over the vegetables and top with the breadcrumbs. Bake for 25–30 minutes, or until the sauce is lightly browned.

Remove from the oven and allow to sit for 10 minutes before serving.

BEST IN: AUTUMN, WINTER & SPRING

Beetroot & carrot casserole

SERVES 4–6

Beetroot and carrots are said to have healing properties for the gut. Serve with poppadoms and steamed basmati rice. –VV

500 g (1 lb 2 oz) bunch of yellow beetroot (beets), with leaves

400 g (14 oz) bunch of baby heirloom carrots

2 tablespoons coconut oil

1 teaspoon ground cumin

1 teaspoon cumin seeds

1 teaspoon fennel seeds

1 teaspoon ground coriander

4 whole cloves

1 cinnamon stick

2 tablespoons finely chopped ginger

2 tablespoons crushed fresh garlic

4 spring (green) onions, finely sliced

handful of chopped coriander (cilantro), to garnish

Trim the tops off the beetroot, reserving the leaves. Peel the bulbs and cut them into eighths; you may want to pop on a pair of food-handling gloves while doing this, so your fingers don't become stained. Wash the leaves well, then roughly chop and set aside. Trim the carrots, scrub them well and set aside also.

Heat the coconut oil in a large heavy-based saucepan over medium heat. Add the ground cumin, cumin seeds, fennel seeds, ground coriander, cloves and cinnamon stick. Cook, stirring constantly, for 2 minutes, or until aromatic.

Add the ginger, garlic and spring onion and stir for a further 1 minute. Add the beetroot, beetroot leaves and carrots. Stir in 60 ml (¼ cup) water, increase the heat and bring to the boil for 5 minutes.

Reduce the heat to a simmer, then cover and cook for a further 20 minutes, or until the beetroot is tender.

Garnish with coriander and serve.

BEST IN: AUTUMN & WINTER

ALREADY VEGAN!

Spiced roasted baby carrot salad with kaffir coconut dressing

SERVES 4

In the cooler months, beautiful earthy heirloom carrots make a lovely warm salad, coupled with a zesty Asian-inspired dressing. This dish also works well in warmer months as a cold salad offering. –VV

500 g (1 lb 2 oz) tri-colour heirloom baby carrots

2 tablespoons coconut oil, melted

1 teaspoon ground cumin

½ teaspoon ground coriander

½ teaspoon ground ginger

½ teaspoon sea salt

30 g (1 oz/¼ cup) slivered almonds, toasted

coriander (cilantro) sprigs, to garnish

KAFFIR COCONUT DRESSING

125 ml (½ cup) coconut cream

2 teaspoons kaffir lime juice

1 teaspoon kaffir lime zest

1½ tablespoons grated palm sugar

¼ teaspoon finely chopped garlic

1 tablespoon vegan fish sauce

½ teaspoon finely chopped red chilli

Preheat the oven to 180°C/350°F (fan-forced). Line a baking tray with baking paper.

Trim the leafy green tops off the carrots, leaving 2 cm (¾ in) of the stalks attached. Wash and scrub the carrots well, then place in a large bowl. Add the coconut oil, cumin, coriander, ginger and salt, tossing thoroughly with your hands until coated.

Transfer the carrots (and any excess coating) to the baking tray and roast for 30–35 minutes, or until the carrots are tender.

Meanwhile, in a small bowl, whisk together the dressing ingredients. Set aside.

Arrange the roasted carrots on a serving platter. Season with salt and freshly ground black pepper. Give the dressing another quick stir and drizzle over the carrots. Scatter with the toasted almonds, garnish with coriander and serve immediately.

BEST IN: AUTUMN, WINTER & SPRING

ALREADY VEGAN!

Lotus root chips

SERVES 4

These fantastic-looking chips are a great snack that are best made close to serving, as they will soften slightly. You can crisp them up in the oven, if needed, by spreading them on a baking tray and baking at 150°C/300°F (fan-forced) for 5 minutes.

If you don't have any togarashi seasoning, simply sprinkle the chips with a little extra sea salt. –CG

1 litre (4 cups) sunflower or peanut oil, for deep-frying

500 g (1 lb 2 oz) section of fresh lotus root (see Note)

salt flakes, for sprinkling

togarashi seasoning, for sprinkling

ALREADY VEGAN!

Pour the oil into a deep-fryer, or into a large deep heavy-based saucepan to no more than one-third full. Heat the oil to 160°C (320°F) on a cooking thermometer.

While the oil is heating, peel the lotus root and slice very finely – about 2 mm (⅛ inch) thick is ideal. Pat dry with paper towel or a clean tea towel.

Working in batches of 10 or so, deep-fry the lotus root slices for 1–2 minutes, or until just turning golden. Transfer to paper towel to drain and sprinkle immediately with a little salt and togarashi.

Repeat with the remaining lotus root slices, then serve immediately.

BEST IN: WINTER

NOTE: If lotus root is unavailable fresh, you can buy frozen lotus root from Asian grocery stores. Thaw before using.

Lotus root, water chestnut & edamame stir-fry

SERVES 4

Lotus root looks amazing and has a fantastic texture. If fresh lotus root is out of season, you can buy packets of the frozen sliced variety from Asian grocery stores. Thaw the slices before cooking.

This stir-fry is delicious with steamed brown rice and steamed Asian greens, such as choy sum, Chinese broccoli or mustard greens. –CG

3 spring (green) onions

80 ml (⅓ cup) Shaoxing rice wine or dry sherry

1 tablespoon soy sauce

1 teaspoon sesame oil

1 teaspoon Chinkiang vinegar (Chinese black vinegar), optional

1 tablespoon peanut oil

2 red Asian shallots, finely sliced

3 cm (1¼ in) piece of ginger, peeled and julienned

2 garlic cloves, finely sliced

400 g (14 oz) section of fresh lotus root, peeled and cut into 5 mm (¼ in) slices

150 g (5½ oz) tin water chestnuts, drained and sliced

140 g (5 oz/1 cup) frozen podded edamame (young green soy beans), thawed

Cut the white section of the spring onions into 4 cm (1½ in) lengths, and the green sections thinly on the diagonal. Soak the green bits in a small bowl of cold water until needed.

In a small bowl or jug, whisk together the rice wine, soy sauce, sesame oil and vinegar, if using. Set aside.

Heat the peanut oil in a wok over medium–high heat until smoking. Stir-fry the shallot, ginger, garlic and white spring onion lengths for 1 minute, or until nicely fragrant.

Add the sliced lotus root and water chestnuts and stir-fry for 1 minute, then add the edamame and toss for 1 minute.

Add the rice wine mixture and stir-fry for another 1–2 minutes, until heated through and fragrant.

Serve immediately, scattered with the drained spring onion greens.

BEST IN: WINTER

ALREADY VEGAN!

Celeriac & lemon mash with mustard & buttermilk

SERVES 4

Adding celeriac to mashed potatoes adds great texture and flavour. This mash with its lemony tang is a delicious accompaniment to roasted mushrooms and hearty bean and legume dishes. For those who are not solely plant-based, it is lovely with grilled fresh fish too. –CG

600 g (1 lb 5 oz) Dutch cream or other mashing potatoes, peeled

1 celeriac, about 500 g (1 lb 2 oz), peeled and chopped

20 g (¾ oz) butter

3 teaspoons wholegrain mustard

1 tablespoon lemon juice

80 ml (⅓ cup) buttermilk, approximately

freshly ground white pepper, to taste

extra virgin olive oil, for drizzling

micro herbs, to garnish

lemon zest shreds, to garnish

Bring a large saucepan of water to the boil and set a large steamer on top. Add the potato and celeriac to the steamer basket, then cover and steam for 10–12 minutes, or until very tender.

Leave to cool slightly, then transfer to a food processor. Add the butter, mustard, lemon juice and most of the buttermilk and pulse until combined – do not over-process, as a bit of texture is desirable. Add a little more buttermilk if necessary, then season to taste with salt and white pepper.

Serve immediately, drizzled with a little olive oil, and scattered with micro herbs and lemon zest.

BEST IN: WINTER

MAKE IT VEGAN!
Replace the butter with olive oil and and use oat milk instead of buttermilk.

Celeriac & rocket remoulade with aquafaba mayo

SERVES 4–6

This simple salad is excellent served with grilled vegetables. To mix things up, add a bit of shredded sweet potato along with the celeriac – it is surprisingly good raw when finely cut. –CG

2 tablespoons hazelnuts

1 celeriac, about 500 g (1 lb 2 oz), peeled

1 teaspoon sea salt (optional)

2 teaspoons lemon juice (optional)

freshly ground white pepper, to taste

large handful of rocket (arugula) leaves

AQUAFABA MAYO

2 teaspoons drained tinned chickpeas (reserve the liquid)

50 ml (1¾ fl oz) aquafaba (the reserved liquid from the chickpeas)

2 teaspoons vegan dijon mustard

2 teaspoons lemon juice

180 ml (⅔ cup) mild olive oil

To make the aquafaba mayo, blitz the chickpeas, aquafaba, mustard and lemon juice with a stick blender until smooth. Add the oil gradually until a creamy emulsion forms. Season to taste. This recipe will make about 250 g (9 oz/1 cup) of mayo. Store in an airtight container in the fridge for up to 7 days.

Preheat the oven to 160°C/320°F (fan-forced). Spread the hazelnuts over a baking tray and bake for 8–10 minutes, or until the skins begin to loosen. Remove from the oven and rub off the skins in a clean tea towel. Roughly chop the nuts and set aside.

Cut the celeriac into long thin strips using a sharp knife, or with a mandoline if you have one. Now taste the celeriac: if it has any bitterness, toss it in a large bowl with the salt and lemon juice, set aside for 30 minutes, then rinse and dry well with paper towel. If the celeriac isn't bitter, simply skip this step and place it straight into a large bowl.

Add enough of the mayo to the celeriac strips to coat them generously, season with white pepper and toss to combine well. Cover and refrigerate for 2–3 hours, or overnight, to soften slightly; the mixture will keep refrigerated in an airtight container for up to 3 days.

Just before serving, mix the rocket through. Serve scattered with the hazelnuts.

BEST IN: WINTER

ALREADY VEGAN!

Raw beetroot relish with sesame

MAKES ABOUT 2 CUPS

Refreshing and slightly tangy, with a bit of crunch, this fresh relish is beautiful served on top of leafy green salads and frittatas, and in lieu of cabbage or coleslaw in tacos. –VV

2 tablespoons sesame oil

2 tablespoons lemon juice

½ teaspoon finely chopped ginger

1 teaspoon mirin

2 beetroot (beets), about 700 g (1 lb 9 oz) in total

500 g (1 lb 2 oz) bunch of radishes

4 spring (green) onions

1 teaspoon coriander seeds

2 tablespoons sesame seeds

dill sprigs, to garnish

In a small bowl, whisk together the sesame oil, lemon juice, ginger and mirin. Season to taste with salt and freshly ground black pepper.

Wearing food-handling gloves, to avoid your fingers staining, peel the beetroot, then grate it into a mixing bowl. Grate the radishes and finely slice the spring onions then add them to the bowl.

Pour the dressing over and mix thoroughly. Cover and place in the fridge for at least 30 minutes before serving, or up to 2 days.

Just before serving, toast the coriander seeds in a small dry frying pan over high heat for 1 minute, tossing regularly so they don't burn. Tip into a small bowl and lightly crush them. Add the sesame seeds to the pan and fry them, tossing frequently, for 1–2 minutes, or until nicely toasted.

Transfer the relish to a serving bowl and sprinkle with the toasted coriander and sesame seeds. Garnish with dill sprigs and serve.

BEST IN: AUTUMN & WINTER

ALREADY VEGAN!

Celeriac, brown onion & mustard tart

SERVES 4

This beautiful tart makes a simple but elegant starter. It is equally lovely as a main – simply double the quantities. Enjoy with a glass of crisp white wine, and a leafy green salad dressed in a balsamic vinaigrette. –VV

1 frozen puff pastry sheet, thawed

2 tablespoons olive oil, plus extra for drizzling

2 brown onions, finely sliced

60 ml (¼ cup) lemon juice

½ small celeriac, peeled

125 g (4½ oz/½ cup) crème fraîche

50 g (1¾ oz/⅓ cup) crumbled goat's cheese

1 tablespoon lemon zest

1 teaspoon wholegrain mustard

2 fresh rosemary sprigs, leaves picked

Preheat the oven to 200°C/400°F (fan-forced). Line a baking tray with baking paper.

Place the puff pastry on the baking tray and bake for 15 minutes. Remove from the oven and flatten the pastry by placing another baking tray on top. Set aside.

Warm the olive oil in a frying pan over medium heat. Add the onion and sauté for 10 minutes, or until translucent. Set aside.

Put the lemon juice in a bowl with about 500 ml (2 cups) water. Thinly slice the celeriac, using a mandoline on its thinnest setting, or a very sharp knife, adding it to the acidulated water so it doesn't discolour.

Bring a saucepan of water to the boil and set a steamer on top. Drain the celeriac, add to the steamer, then cover and cook for 3–4 minutes, or until tender. Drain and pat dry with paper towel.

Place the crème fraîche, goat's cheese, lemon zest and mustard in a small bowl and mix thoroughly.

Spread three-quarters of the crème fraîche mixture onto the pastry, leaving a 1 cm (½ in) border around the edges. Top with layers of the sautéed onion and celeriac. Using a teaspoon, dollop the remaining crème fraîche mixture on top, along with the rosemary.

Drizzle with a little extra olive oil and bake for 15–20 minutes, until the pastry is golden. Serve immediately.

BEST IN: WINTER

Pan-tossed turnips & nashi with stilton

SERVES 4

Earthy turnips and crunchy nashi pears are a beautiful combination. Paired off with toasted walnuts and sharp stilton, this dish is a fabulous starter. The texture of the nashi pear is important here, but at a pinch a packham or corella pear will stand in nicely. –VV

100 g (3½ oz/1 cup) walnuts

1 tablespoon olive oil

1 brown onion, finely sliced

500 g (1 lb 2 oz) bunch of baby turnips, cut in half

2 nashi pears, cored and cut into 8 wedges each

1 garlic clove, crushed

125 ml (½ cup) dry white wine

40 g (1½ oz) unsalted butter

35 g (1¼ oz/¼ cup) raisins

75 g (2¾ oz/½ cup) crumbled stilton

Preheat the oven to 180°C/350°F (fan-forced). Place the walnuts on a baking tray and toast in the oven for 1 minute. Toss the walnuts and toast for a further 1 minute, then remove from the oven and tip onto a plate to cool completely.

Heat the olive oil in a frying pan over medium heat. Add the onion, turnip, pear and garlic. Cook, stirring occasionally, for 20 minutes, or until the turnip is golden.

Increase the heat to high. Stir in the wine, then leave to boil for 4 minutes. Reduce the heat to a simmer and stir in the butter, raisins and 125 ml (½ cup) water.

Cover and cook for a further 10–15 minutes, or until the turnip is tender. Season with salt and freshly ground black pepper.

Transfer to a serving dish and serve immediately, scattered with the toasted walnuts and stilton.

BEST IN: AUTUMN & WINTER

Roast turnips with goat's cheese & dukkah

SERVES 4 AS A SIDE

The exotic flavours of dukkah add flair to simple roasted turnips, which make a lovely side to frittatas. If serving this as a starter, you can plate each dish individually. Baby turnips are another beautiful option here. –VV

2 medium-sized turnips, peeled and quartered

2 tablespoons olive oil

½ teaspoon sea salt

½ teaspoon freshly ground black pepper

250 g (9 oz) goat's cheese

½ teaspoon finely grated garlic

coriander (cilantro) leaves, to garnish

DUKKAH

1 teaspoon coriander seeds

1 teaspoon cumin seeds

40 g (1½ oz/¼ cup) almonds

1 tablespoon black sesame seeds

1 teaspoon white poppy seeds

1 teaspoon finely grated lime zest

½ teaspoon ground sumac

Preheat the oven to 180°C/350°F (fan-forced). Line a baking tray with baking paper.

Toss the turnips in a bowl with the olive oil, salt and pepper. Transfer to the baking tray and roast for 20–25 minutes, or until tender and browned. Remove from the oven and cover with foil to keep warm.

Meanwhile, prepare the dukkah. Toast the coriander and cumin seeds in a small dry frying pan over high heat for 2 minutes, tossing regularly so they don't burn. Tip into a small bowl.

Lightly toast the almonds in the pan, set aside to cool slightly, then roughly chop.

Using a mortar and pestle, crush the toasted coriander and cumin seeds, and the sesame and poppy seeds to a coarse mixture. Place in a small bowl and mix together with the almonds, lime zest and sumac.

Crumble the goat's cheese into a small bowl. Add the garlic and mix together until smooth.

Smear the goat's cheese onto a serving plate and top with the warm turnips. Sprinkle with the dukkah and a little salt and freshly ground black pepper. Garnish with coriander leaves and serve immediately.

BEST IN: AUTUMN & WINTER

MAKE IT VEGAN!
Either leave out the goat's cheese or replace it with a soft vegan cheese or your favourite hummus.

Daikon pickle

MAKES 1 × 500 ML (2 CUP) JAR

Lively and cleansing, this pickle is fabulous as an appetiser or alongside rich food. Try replacing half the daikon with carrot, and shredding or julienning them both instead of cutting into cubes. –CG

110 g (4 oz/½ cup) caster sugar

180 ml (¾ cup) rice vinegar

pinch of salt

500 g (1 lb 2 oz) daikon radish or Korean radish

3 coriander (cilantro) roots, scraped

ALREADY VEGAN!

Preheat the oven to 180°C/350°F (fan-forced). Wash a 500 ml (2 cup) jar and lid with warm soapy water, rinse well and place in the oven for 30 minutes to sterilise them.

Remove the jar and lid from the oven and set aside until cool enough to handle.

Stir the sugar, vinegar, salt and 180 ml (¾ cup) water together in a jug until dissolved.

Peel the radish and cut into 1 cm (½ in) cubes. Place in the sterilised jar with the coriander roots and pour the vinegar liquid over. Gently stir to combine.

Put the lid on loosely and leave the jar at room temperature for 3–4 hours, stirring occasionally. Seal and label the jar, then move to the refrigerator.

The pickle is ready to enjoy straight away, and will keep in the refrigerator for up to 3 months.

Serve chilled.

BEST IN: AUTUMN

Radish & mango salad

SERVES 4

Peppery radishes, sweet mango and fragrant Vietnamese mint make for a wonderfully light and refreshing summertime salad. –VV

½ teaspoon finely grated lime zest

2 tablespoons lime juice

60 ml (¼ cup) extra virgin olive oil

1½ tablespoons grated palm sugar

¼ teaspoon sea salt

500 g (1 lb 2 oz) bunch of breakfast radishes, halved lengthways

1 mango, peeled and sliced into 1 cm (½ inch) thick wedges

1 long cucumber, peeled lengthways into long thin strips

handful of Vietnamese mint leaves

In a small bowl, whisk together the lime zest, lime juice, olive oil, palm sugar and salt until an emulsion forms.

Layer the radish, mango, cucumber and mint leaves on a platter.

Drizzle the dressing over the salad and serve immediately.

BEST IN: SUMMER

ALREADY VEGAN!

Tubers

Jerusalem artichokes

jicama

potatoes

sweet potatoes

Hasselback potatoes with butter & sage

SERVES 4

Who can resist the extra crunch given to these roasted potatoes with their deeply scored surfaces – not to mention the extra texture from the breadcrumbs and cheese? No wonder these Swedish-style baked potatoes have seen a bit of a resurgence lately. They are a great accompaniment to just about anything. –CG

8 small royal blue or other roasting or all-purpose potatoes, about 1 kg (2 lb 3 oz) in total, left unpeeled

50 g (1¾ oz) butter

2 tablespoons olive oil

2 garlic cloves, finely sliced

small handful of sage leaves

sea salt flakes, for sprinkling

20 g (¾ oz/¼ cup) coarse fresh breadcrumbs

2 tablespoons finely grated parmesan

malt vinegar, for drizzling (optional)

MAKE IT VEGAN!
Use olive oil instead of the butter and swap the parmesan for nutritional yeast.

Preheat the oven to 200°C/400°F (fan-forced). Scrub the potatoes well and set aside to dry.

In a small saucepan, gently heat the butter, oil and garlic until foaming. Add the sage leaves and cook, stirring, for about 2 minutes, or until the leaves are crisp and the garlic is just starting to brown lightly. Remove from the heat. Using a slotted spoon, remove the garlic and sage and drain on paper towel.

Place an unpeeled potato on a chopping board and rest a chopstick next to it, lengthways, on the side closest to you. Using a sharp knife, make thin parallel cuts, at 3–5 mm (⅛–¼ in) intervals, through the potato, down to about three-quarters of the way through, or until you hit the chopstick. The chopstick will stop you cutting all the way through. The closer your cuts, the crispier the result — a great opportunity to practise your knife skills!

Place the cut potatoes in a large roasting tin, sliced side up. Brush generously with about half the browned butter mixture. Sprinkle with sea salt flakes and freshly ground black pepper.

Bake for 30 minutes, then remove from the oven and brush with the remaining butter mixture, ensuring you get plenty in between the slices. Return to the oven for a further 20 minutes, then sprinkle with the breadcrumbs and parmesan.

Bake for a final 10–15 minutes, or until golden and crisp on the outside, and tender in the centre.

Serve immediately, scattered with the crisp sage leaves and garlic, and sprinkled with a drizzle of vinegar if you like.

BEST IN: WINTER & SPRING

Super-crunchy roasted potatoes

SERVES 4

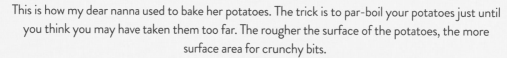

This is how my dear nanna used to bake her potatoes. The trick is to par-boil your potatoes just until you think you may have taken them too far. The rougher the surface of the potatoes, the more surface area for crunchy bits.

This recipe is generous with the olive oil; but you can reduce it to 2 tablespoons, if you must. Life is just better with roasted potatoes. –CG

1 kg (2 lb 3 oz) royal blue or other roasting or all-purpose potatoes, peeled

60 ml (¼ cup) olive oil

sea salt flakes, to taste

ALREADY VEGAN!

Preheat the oven to 200°C/400°F (fan-forced).

Cut the potatoes into roughly 6 cm (2½ in) chunks and place in a large saucepan. Cover with cold water and bring to the boil over medium–high heat. Add a good pinch of salt and boil for 12–15 minutes, or until a skewer can be inserted into a potato chunk relatively easily, and the potato just slides off the skewer when you lift it up. The surface of the potato should just be starting to break down.

Carefully drain the par-boiled potatoes, then return to the pan and place over medium heat. Shake the pan gently over the heat for about 30 seconds to drive off any extra moisture. Drizzle the olive oil into the saucepan and season generously with sea salt flakes. Put the lid on the saucepan and gently shake the pan, holding the lid in place, to coat the potatoes with the olive oil, and to rough up their surfaces.

Tip the potatoes into a shallow roasting tin and spread them out in a single layer. Make sure you scrape out the saucepan well – a silicon spatula is good for this – and add the residue to the roasting tin along with the potatoes. It will turn into the most delightful crunchy bits!

Roast for 45 minutes. Remove from the oven, turn the potatoes over, then roast for a further 10–15 minutes, or until golden and crisp on the outside, and tender in the centre.

Serve immediately.

BEST IN: WINTER & SPRING

Crispy potato stacks

SERVES 4

These tasty little stacks are like individual scalloped potato gratins, with extra crispy bits. And we all know the crispy bits are the best part! –CG

800 g (1 lb 12 oz) russet burbank potatoes, or other varieties suitable for slicing and baking

1 tablespoon chopped lemon thyme

2 teaspoons shredded sage

50 g (1¾ oz) butter, melted, plus extra for greasing

60 ml (¼ cup) thickened (whipping) cream (35% fat)

65 g (2¼ oz/½ cup) grated gruyère or other melting cheese

60 g (2 oz/½ cup) grated mature cheddar

Preheat the oven to 200°C/400°F (fan-forced). Lightly butter a 12-hole, 80 ml (⅓ cup capacity) muffin tray.

Scrub the potatoes clean. Using a mandoline or food processor, thinly slice the potatoes, ideally about 2–3 mm (⅛ in) thick.

Combine the potato slices, herbs and melted butter in a large bowl, gently mixing together with your hands. Season well with salt and freshly ground black pepper. Add the cream and cheeses and toss again.

Stack the potato slices and layer into the muffin holes. Don't worry about trying to be too neat here – they will have a rustic charm about them. The muffin holes will seem rather full, but the potato will shrink as it cooks.

Cover with a sheet of baking paper, then a sheet of foil, sealing the edges under. Place the whole thing on a baking tray, to catch any drips.

Transfer to the oven and bake for 30 minutes. Remove the baking paper and foil and cook for a further 15–20 minutes, or until the potato is tender and well browned.

Remove from the oven and allow to settle for 5 minutes.

Run a small palette knife around the edges of each stack to release them, then lift out carefully. Serve immediately.

BEST IN: WINTER & SPRING

Ann's potato, cheese & onion pie

SERVES 6–8

My excellent British mother-in-law, Ann, is famous for this delicious pie, and is barred from attending any family function unless she comes bearing at least two! Serve with a salad or greens. –CG

800 g (1 lb 12 oz) Toolangi delight or other mashing potatoes, chopped into 6 cm (2½ in) chunks

300 g (10½ oz/2½ cups) grated mature cheddar

2 onions, grated

freshly ground white pepper, to taste

1 free-range egg, beaten

SOUR CREAM PASTRY

300 g (10½ oz/2 cups) plain (all-purpose) flour, plus extra for dusting

200 g (7 oz) very cold unsalted butter, diced

125 g (4½ oz/½ cup) sour cream, approximately

To make the pastry, put the flour and butter in a food processor and pulse until the mixture resembles coarse breadcrumbs. Add the sour cream and continue to pulse until the dough starts to cling together. Do not over-process – the dough does not need to form a ball. Add a little more sour cream if the mixture seems dry.

Tip the pastry mixture onto a clean work surface and press together into a disc. Wrap in plastic wrap and refrigerate for 20 minutes.

Meanwhile, preheat the oven to 180°C/350°F (fan-forced).

Roll two-thirds of the chilled pastry on a lightly floured surface to 4 mm (¼ inch) thick. Take a pie dish measuring 20 cm (8 in) across the base and ease the pastry into the dish, leaving the dough overhanging the edge. Chill for 15–20 minutes.

Meanwhile, boil, steam or microwave the potato until tender. Mash until smooth, then set aside in a large bowl to cool slightly. Stir in the cheese and onion and season with salt and ground white pepper.

Spoon the potato filling evenly into the lined pie dish.

Roll the remaining pastry to about 4 mm (¼ in) thick, large enough to cover the pie. Leave it in one piece, if you'd like to keep things simple. Brush the edge of the pastry in the dish with the beaten egg, and then lay the pastry sheet over the top. Gently press the edges together, then trim with a knife. Crimp the edges with your fingers or a fork, then brush the top of the pie with the beaten egg. Decorate the top of the pie, if you like, by cutting out decorative leaves or shapes from the remaining dough and arranging them on top. Brush the top with more egg. (Alternatively, you can cut the top sheet of pastry into 1.5 cm/½ inch strips and form a lattice over the pie.)

Place the pie on a baking tray and bake for 40–45 minutes, or until the pastry is cooked through and the top is golden brown. Remove from the oven and leave to rest for 10 minutes or so, then cut into slices and serve.

BEST IN: WINTER & SPRING

Potato, cheddar & jalapeño croquettes

MAKES 14

These are terrific served as a starter, or as a snack alongside a round of margaritas. With their crunchy exterior, smoky croquet base and sharp, spicy centre, these enticing morsels will be devoured very quickly. –VV

800 g (1 lb 12 oz) sebago or other mashing potatoes, washed well but not peeled

2 tablespoons smoked paprika

1 tablespoon fine sea salt

20 g (¾ oz) unsalted butter

60 ml (¼ cup) thickened (whipping) cream (35% fat)

35 g (1¼ oz/¼ cup) plain (all-purpose) flour, plus extra for dusting

120 g (4½ oz) cheddar, cut into 2 cm × 1 cm (¾ in × ½ in) blocks

2 jalapeño chillies, deseeded and finely chopped

2 free-range eggs

100 g (3½ oz/1 cup) fine dry breadcrumbs

vegetable oil, for shallow-frying

Place the potatoes in a saucepan and three-quarters fill with water. Bring to the boil over high heat and leave to cook for 20–25 minutes, or until cooked through when tested with a skewer.

Drain the potatoes in a colander. When cool enough to handle, remove the skins with a paring knife. Place the potatoes back in the pan and add the paprika, salt, butter and cream. Mash roughly using a spoon, then pass through a potato ricer, into a bowl.

Chill the mash in the fridge for 1 hour, or until completely cold.

Tip the flour onto a plate and remove the mash from the fridge. Using floured hands, scoop 2 tablespoons of the mash into your palm and gently press it into a flat patty. Place two pieces of cheese and some jalapeño chilli in the middle, then close your hand to encase the filling with the mash. Gently form into a croquet shape, then roll in the flour and set aside on a clean tray. Repeat until all the mash is used up.

Chill the croquettes in the fridge for another 2 hours.

Beat the eggs in a shallow bowl. Spread the breadcrumbs over a flat plate.

Pour 4 cm (1½ in) of vegetable oil into a small frying pan. Heat over medium heat until a cooking thermometer registers 180°C (350°F), or until a cube of bread dropped into the oil turns golden brown in 15 seconds.

Working in batches, dip the croquettes one by one into the egg, then roll in the breadcrumbs. Gently lower into the hot oil and cook, turning regularly, for 3–4 minutes, until golden brown. Remove using a slotted spoon and briefly drain on paper towel.

Serve immediately.

BEST IN: AUTUMN, WINTER & SPRING

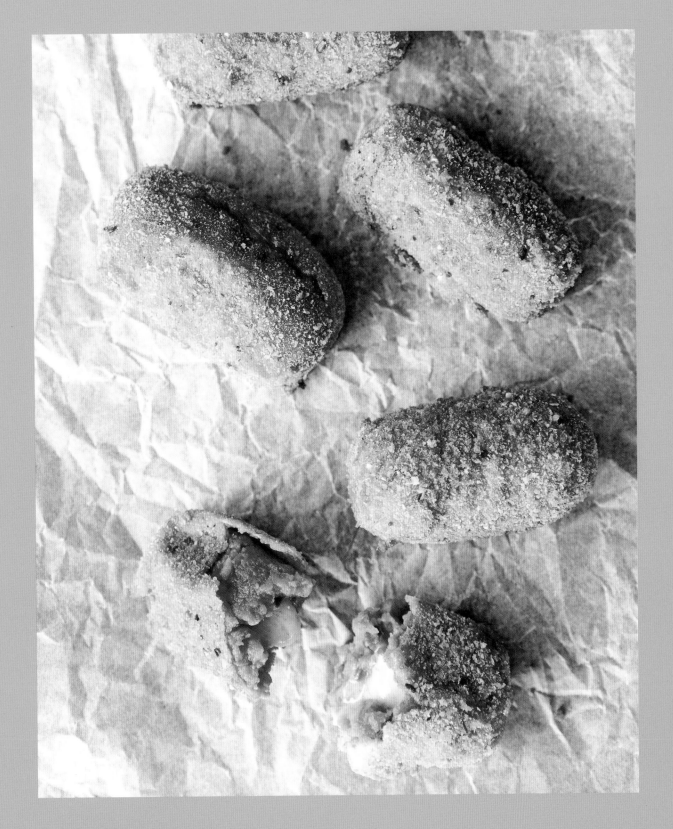

Sweet potato gnocchi with sage burnt butter

SERVES 6

For the best results here, you really need to roast your potatoes. Roasting provides a dry flesh that is smooth to handle and retains all the sweet, nutty goodness from the potatoes. –VV

2 orange sweet potatoes, about 700 g (1 lb 9 oz) in total, scrubbed

2 desiree or other baking potatoes, about 300 g (10½ oz) in total, scrubbed

olive oil, for drizzling

1 tablespoon table salt

35 g (1¼ oz/⅓ cup) finely grated parmesan, plus extra to serve

1 large free-range egg, beaten

1 tablespoon honey

about 300 g (10½ oz/2 cups) plain (all-purpose) flour, plus extra for dusting

SAGE BURNT BUTTER

140 g (5 oz) unsalted butter

20 sage leaves

1 teaspoon freshly grated nutmeg

1 garlic clove, crushed

Preheat the oven to 180°C/350°F (fan-forced). Line a baking tray with baking paper. Leaving the skins on, cut the sweet potatoes and potatoes in half lengthways. Drizzle with olive oil and season with 2 teaspoons of the salt. Place cut side down on the baking tray and bake for 25–30 minutes, or until a skewer passes through the potatoes easily. Remove from the oven and leave to cool.

Using a spoon, scoop out the potato and sweet potato flesh, discarding the skins. Pass the flesh through a potato ricer, into a mixing bowl. Stir in the remaining 2 teaspoons salt, along with the parmesan, egg and honey. Working slowly, add the flour in batches, mixing thoroughly until a dough forms that doesn't stick to your hand; you may not need all the flour.

Turn the dough out onto a lightly floured surface and roll out into a small log shape. Using a sharp knife, cut the log into eight equal pieces. Roll each piece into a 1 cm (½ in) thick 'rope', then cut each one into 1 cm (½ in) 'pillows'. If you like, you can roll the gnocchi pillows with a fork to create the classic indents.

Bring a large saucepan of water to the boil. Working in batches, cook the gnocchi for 20–30 seconds, or until they float to the surface. Remove with a slotted spoon, onto a sheet of baking paper, and set aside.

For the sage burnt butter, melt the butter in a large frying pan over medium heat for 2–3 minutes, until it begins to foam. Add the sage and cook for 1 minute, or until crisp. Remove the sage and set aside on paper towel.

Continue cooking the butter for 1–2 minutes, until brown. Immediately remove from the heat and add the gnocchi, followed by the nutmeg, garlic and 60 ml (¼ cup) warm water. Place the frying pan back over medium heat for 2–3 minutes, tossing to coat the gnocchi and warm them through. Serve immediately, garnished with the fried sage leaves, and a sprinkling of black pepper and extra parmesan.

BEST IN: AUTUMN

Sweet potato & corn empanadas

MAKES 20

These tasty hand-held pies are great finger food for a party or as an appetiser. They can be made up to a day in advance and stored, covered well in the fridge before baking them just before needed. Or, double the batch and freeze them, ready to bake at a moment's notice. They'll keep for up to a month in a sealed container in the freezer. –CG

1 tablespoon olive oil

1 onion, chopped

kernels from 1 fresh corn cob

300 g (10½ oz) sweet potato, peeled and cut into 1 cm (½ in) chunks

4 garlic cloves, crushed

1 teaspoon chopped thyme

1 tablespoon tomato paste (concentrated purée)

2 teaspoons sweet smoked paprika

125 ml (½ cup) Vegetable stock (see page 23)

3 spring (green) onions, finely sliced

80 g (2¾ oz/½ cup) chopped pitted green olives

2 tablespoons chopped parsley

2 hard-boiled free-range eggs, cooled and grated

1 free-range egg, beaten with 1 tablespoon water

DOUGH

60 g (2 oz) butter, melted

1 teaspoon salt

485 g (1 lb 1 oz/3¼ cups) plain (all-purpose) flour, plus extra for dusting

1 teaspoon baking powder

GREEN SAUCE

80 ml (⅓ cup) olive oil

4 spring (green) onions, roughly chopped

1 teaspoon ground cumin

1 teaspoon ground coriander

2 large handfuls of coriander (cilantro), roughly chopped

1 jalapeño chilli, roughly chopped

finely grated zest of 1 lime

2 tablespoons lime juice

To make the dough, combine the butter and salt in a large mixing bowl. Add 250 ml (1 cup) water and stir to dissolve the salt. Gradually stir in the flour until the dough comes together. Knead in the bowl for 1–2 minutes, until firm and smooth, adding a little more flour if sticky. Form into a flat disc and cover with plastic wrap. Refrigerate for 1 hour.

Meanwhile, get started on the filling. Heat the olive oil in a large heavy-based frying pan with a lid over medium heat. Add the onion and corn kernels and cook, stirring occasionally, for 8–10 minutes, or until the onion and corn are softened and lightly browned.

Add the sweet potato, garlic and thyme and mix well. Stir in the tomato paste and paprika. Cook, stirring, for 1 minute, then stir in the stock, scraping and dissolving the tasty bits sticking to the pan. Cover and simmer for about 10 minutes, until the sweet potato is tender and the stock mostly evaporated.

Remove from the heat and stir in the spring onion, olives and parsley. Season with salt and freshly ground black pepper. Set aside to cool, then refrigerate until required.

Preheat the oven to 170°C/340°F (fan-forced). Line two baking trays with baking paper.

Divide the chilled dough into 20 pieces and form into balls. Working with four or five balls at a time, roll them out on a lightly floured surface into 12 cm (4¾ inch) circles.

Put a heaped tablespoon of filling in the centre of the rounds, adding a little grated hard-boiled egg to the top of each. Moisten the outer edge of the rounds with water. Fold the dough over the filling to form half-moons, pressing the edges together. Roll or pinch the edges into little pleats, or crimp them together with a fork. Repeat with the remaining dough and filling.

Place the empanadas on the baking trays. Brush the tops lightly with the beaten egg mixture. Bake for 15–18 minutes, until well browned.

Meanwhile, combine the green sauce ingredients in a processor or blender and whiz together until smooth. Gradually add up to 60 ml (¼ cup) water, until you reach the desired consistency. Transfer to a small bowl.

Serve the empanadas warm, with the green sauce.

BEST IN: AUTUMN

Sweet potato & celeriac bake

SERVES 4

Here is one deliciously creamy bake. It may be a little bit messy and fiddly layering the vegetables and placing them on their sides, but it is worth the effort – the end result looks impressive and gives you extra crispy bits.

If you don't have the time, simply lay the vegetables flat and your bake will still work out fine. –CG

20 g (¾ oz) butter, plus extra for greasing

1 tablespoon olive oil

1 leek, white and pale green parts only, finely sliced

2 garlic cloves, finely sliced

1 large orange sweet potato, scrubbed

1 celeriac, about 500 g (1 lb 2 oz), peeled

500 ml (2 cups) thickened (whipping) cream (35% fat)

130 g (4½ oz/1 cup) grated gruyère

Preheat the oven to 180°C/350°F (fan-forced). Lightly butter a 2 litre (8 cup capacity) shallow baking dish.

Place the butter and oil in a large heavy-based frying pan over medium heat. Add the leek and cook, stirring, for 5–6 minutes, until tender. Add the garlic and cook until fragrant.

Meanwhile, slice the sweet potato and celeriac as finely as you can – about 1–2 mm (¹⁄₁₆–⅛ in) – using a food processor, or a mandoline if you have one. Set aside.

Stir the cream into the sautéed leek mixture. Season well with salt and freshly ground black pepper, bring to the boil, then remove from the heat. Add the potato and celeriac slices and mix until well combined. Set aside to cool slightly.

Using your hands, gather the vegetables into piles and layer them into the baking dish, so that they are sitting vertically. Pack them evenly into the dish.

Cover with foil and bake for 40 minutes. Remove the foil, sprinkle with the cheese and bake for a further 30–35 minutes, or until the potato and celeriac are tender and well browned on top.

Remove from the oven and allow to settle for 5 minutes before serving.

BEST IN: AUTUMN & WINTER

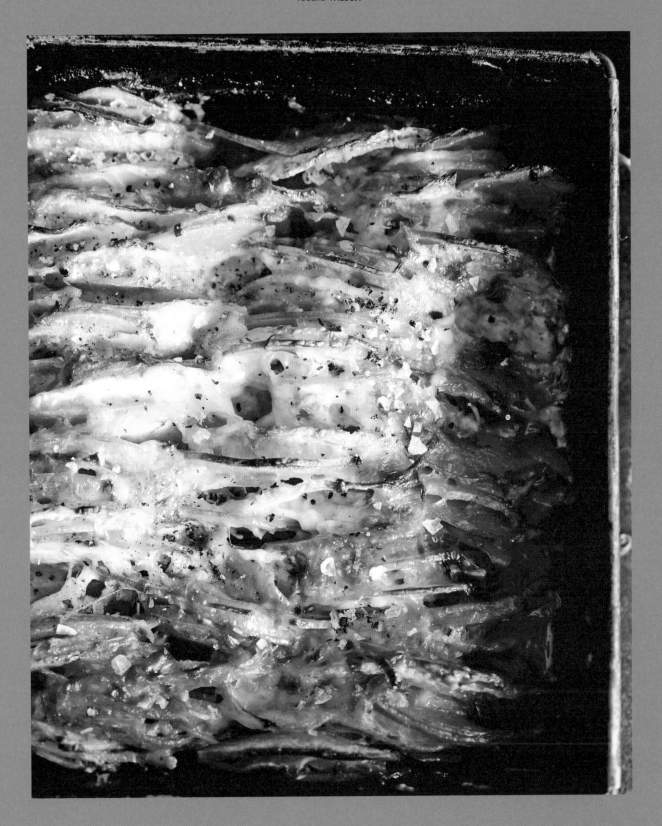

Whole baked sweet potatoes with lentils, feta & olives

SERVES 4

Use any sweet potatoes for this recipe, or a mix of different varieties. Serve as a main meal with salad and a good dollop of natural yoghurt. Any leftovers can be eaten cold the next day. –CG

4 sweet potatoes, about 300 g (10½ oz) each

100 g (3½ oz/½ cup) Puy lentils (tiny blue-green lentils), rinsed and drained

100 g (3½ oz) large green olives, pitted and sliced

1 small tomato, chopped

1 tablespoon baby capers

100 g (3½ oz) feta, crumbled

small handful of parsley or basil, roughly torn, plus extra to serve

1 tablespoon extra virgin olive oil

rocket (arugula) leaves, to serve

MAKE IT VEGAN!
Use vegan feta or add some diced avocado instead.

Preheat the oven to 180°C/350°F (fan-forced).

Scrub the sweet potatoes well, leaving the skin on. Pierce each one several times with a fork, then place them directly on an oven rack in the centre of the oven, with a baking tray below to catch any drips. Bake for 50–60 minutes, until very tender when pierced with a skewer. Remove from the oven and set aside to cool slightly.

Meanwhile, cook the lentils in a small saucepan of boiling water for 25–30 minutes, until tender. Drain well and place in a bowl. Add the olives, tomato and capers. Mix gently.

Cut the sweet potatoes lengthways down the centre, about three-quarters of the way through, and squeeze the ends gently to open them out. Remove a spoonful of flesh from each sweet potato, mash roughly, then gently stir through the lentil mixture with a little salt and freshly ground black pepper. Lastly, add the feta and herbs and gently fold until just combined.

Fill the sweet potatoes with the lentil mixture and drizzle with the olive oil.

Serve immediately, scattered with extra herbs, some rocket leaves on the side, and a dollop of yoghurt if you like.

BEST IN: AUTUMN

Roast sweet potato with miso & ginger caramel

SERVES 4

For this recipe, you can use a combination of orange and white sweet potato for added visual effect, and for their slightly different textures. If they cook through before they have browned quite enough, place them under the grill (broiler) for a few more minutes. Any leftovers can be added to a hearty salad the following day. –CG

60 g (2 oz) unsalted butter

2 tablespoons white miso paste (shiro miso)

2 tablespoons honey

2 teaspoons finely grated ginger

2 teaspoons rice vinegar

2 large sweet potatoes, about 1 kg (2 lb 3 oz) in total, scrubbed

1 spring (green) onion, sliced

roasted black sesame seeds, to serve

Preheat the oven to 190°C/375°F (fan-forced). Line a large roasting tin with baking paper.

Combine the butter, miso paste and honey in a small saucepan over medium heat. Cook, stirring, for 2–3 minutes, or until the butter has melted and the mixture is combined and smooth. Stir in the ginger and vinegar and remove from the heat.

Leaving the skin on, cut the sweet potatoes into wedges and place in the roasting tin. Drizzle the miso mixture over and toss to combine. Spread the sweet potatoes out in a single layer.

Transfer to the oven and bake, turning the potatoes over once or twice, for 30–35 minutes, or until tender when pierced with a skewer.

Serve warm, scattered with the spring onion and sesame seeds.

BEST IN: AUTUMN

Jerusalem artichoke & potato frittata

SERVES 4–6

The beautifully coloured skin of the royal blue potatoes is such an elegant feature of this dish. You'll need to slice the potato and artichokes very thinly; a mandoline is perfect for this, and makes the job quick and easy. This lovely frittata can be served warm or cold, perhaps with a crisp baby cos (romaine) lettuce salad. It's the perfect traveller, well suited to picnics. –VV

3 royal blue potatoes, about 250 g (9 oz) in total, scrubbed

300 g (10½ oz) Jerusalem artichokes, washed but not peeled

60 g (2 oz) unsalted butter

1 tablespoon lemon zest

6 large sage leaves

6 free-range eggs

1 teaspoon sea salt

1 teaspoon freshly ground black pepper

4 garlic cloves, crushed

1 tablespoon thyme leaves

Preheat the oven to 180°C/350°F (fan-forced).

Using a mandoline, slice the potatoes as thinly as possible – about 1 mm (1/16 inch) thick. Do the same with the Jerusalem artichokes and set aside.

In a medium-sized, non-stick, ovenproof saucepan, melt the butter and lemon zest over medium heat. Tip the mixture into a small bowl and set aside.

Place the pan back over low heat. Arrange the sage leaves around the base of the pan, in a circular pattern. Add half the potato slices, overlapping them to create a fanned base, then brush with the melted butter mixture. Layer all the Jerusalem artichoke slices over the potatoes, overlapping them again, and brushing them with the melted butter mixture. Overlap the remaining potato slices on top, brushing with the remaining melted butter mixture.

Put the lid on and leave to simmer for 5 minutes.

Beat the eggs in a bowl, with the salt, pepper, garlic and thyme. Gently and evenly pour the egg mixture over the potatoes, shaking the pan to distribute the egg. Put the lid on and continue cooking for 2 minutes.

Transfer the covered saucepan to the oven and cook the frittata for 10–15 minutes, or until the potato is tender when tested with a skewer.

Remove from the oven and allow the frittata to settle in the pan for 15 minutes.

Flip the frittata onto a serving dish, so the sage leaves are presented on top.

BEST IN: AUTUMN & WINTER

Jerusalem artichoke soup with chunky sourdough croutons & hazelnuts

SERVES 4

Jerusalem artichokes are at their peak in autumn and winter. Their earthiness and distinct flavour pairs particularly well with sage and thyme. This soup makes an elegant starter for a cool-weather dinner party. —CG

2½ tablespoons olive oil

1 onion, chopped

2 garlic cloves, finely sliced

750 g (1 lb 11 oz) Jerusalem artichokes,
peeled and sliced

1 desiree or other all-purpose potato,
peeled and chopped

1 thyme sprig, plus some extra leaves
to garnish

1 sage sprig

500–750 ml (2–3 cups) Vegetable stock
(see page 23)

lemon juice or sherry vinegar, to taste

60 ml (¼ cup) pouring (single/light)
cream (optional)

SOURDOUGH CROUTONS

2 thick slices light rye sourdough bread,
about 100 g (3½ oz) in total

2½ tablespoons olive oil

small handful of sage leaves

1 tablespoon hazelnuts, roughly chopped

MAKE IT VEGAN!
Leave out
the cream.

Heat the olive oil in a large saucepan over low–medium heat. Add the onion and garlic and cook, stirring occasionally, for 5 minutes, or until softened. Add the artichoke and potato and cook, stirring occasionally, for 3–5 minutes, or until the vegetables just start to colour and caramelise.

Add the thyme and sage sprigs, and enough stock to just cover the vegetables. Stir well. Bring to the boil, reduce the heat and simmer gently, partially covered, for 20 minutes, or until the vegetables are tender.

Remove from the heat, remove the herb sprigs, and leave to cool slightly. Blend or process the mixture until smooth.

Pass the mixture through a sieve into a clean pan, discarding any solids if you like a supremely smooth soup. Add the lemon juice or sherry vinegar and season with salt and freshly ground black pepper. Stir in the cream, if using, and gently reheat the soup.

Meanwhile, for the croutons, roughly tear the bread into 1.5 cm (½ in) chunks, leaving the crusts on. Heat the oil in a large heavy-based frying pan over medium heat. Add the sage leaves to the pan, briefly cook until crisp, then remove with a slotted spoon and drain on paper towel. Add the bread and hazelnuts to the pan. Cook, stirring occasionally, for 5 minutes, or until the bread is well browned and crisp, and the hazelnuts have taken on some colour.

Serve the soup immediately, scattered with the croutons, crisp sage leaves and hazelnuts, and a sprinkling of extra thyme.

BEST IN: AUTUMN & WINTER

Dill fettuccine with Jerusalem artichoke

SERVES 6

The skin of the Jerusalem artichoke is surprisingly flavoursome. Many recipes call for peeling these little beauties – but instead just scrub them and keep the skin intact for a full flavour experience. –VV

300 g (10½ oz) Jerusalem artichokes, scrubbed

40 g (1½ oz) unsalted butter

2 tablespoons olive oil

60 ml (¼ cup) lemon juice

½ teaspoon lemon zest

dill sprigs, to garnish

shaved parmesan, to garnish

FETTUCCINE DOUGH

600 g (1 lb 5 oz) '00' pasta flour (see Note), plus extra for dusting

6 free-range eggs

2 tablespoons finely chopped dill

To make the dough, sift the flour into a large bowl and make a well in the centre. Beat the eggs, then add to the flour with the dill and 2 tablespoons water. Using your hands, gently combine until a dough forms. Turn out onto a lightly floured surface and knead for 8 minutes, or until the dough is smooth and free of lumps. Wrap in plastic wrap and leave to rest at room temperature for 40 minutes.

Cut the rested dough into eight portions. Using a pasta machine, roll out the dough, starting from the thickest fettuccine setting, through to the second thinnest. Finish on the thinnest setting. Roll the pasta into loose nests, set aside on a floured tray and cover with a dry tea towel.

Slice the Jerusalem artichokes into 5 mm (¼ in) rounds and set aside. Melt the butter and olive oil in a large frying pan with a lid over medium heat. Increase the heat to high and add the Jerusalem artichoke slices, lemon juice and zest. Cook for 2 minutes, then reduce the heat to low. Cover and simmer for a further 10 minutes, or until the artichoke is tender and browned.

Meanwhile, bring a large saucepan of salted water to the boil. Add the fettuccine and cook for 4–5 minutes, or until it floats to the surface. Drain, reserving about 125 ml (½ cup) of the pasta water.

When the artichoke is tender, increase the heat to medium and add the pasta. Gently toss to coat the pasta in the sauce, adding a little pasta water until the sauce thickens. Leave to simmer for 2 minutes, then remove from the heat and season with salt and freshly ground black pepper. Serve immediately, garnished with dill and parmesan.

BEST IN: WINTER

NOTE: '00' flour (or 'tipo 00' flour) is more finely milled than plain (all-purpose) flour, giving a softer, lighter and airier result in pasta, bread and pizza doughs. Many commercially milled flours are labelled 'cake', 'bread' or 'pastry' flour, to help guide their use. Using a 'pastry' flour, if possible, will give a more delicate result here.

Jicama & green papaya rice paper rolls

SERVES 5

The refreshing crunch of jicama adds lovely texture to these rice paper rolls. They are best made just before serving, so this is the perfect excuse for gathering some extra hands in the kitchen to help with the rolling. If your local Asian grocer doesn't stock brown rice paper wrappers, just use the regular white wrappers instead. –VV

100 g (3½ oz) packet rice vermicelli noodles

1 medium-sized jicama

1 small green papaya

1 carrot

small handful of coriander (cilantro), shredded

small handful of mint leaves, shredded

10 square brown rice paper wrappers

LIME, CHILLI & SHOYU DRESSING

juice of ½ lime

2 tablespoons nama shoyu ('raw' shoyu) or soy sauce

1 tablespoon vegan fish sauce, optional

1 red chilli, thinly sliced

1 teaspoon grated palm sugar

LIME, GINGER & PEANUT DIPPING SAUCE

170 ml (⅔ cup) hoisin sauce

90 g (3 oz/⅓ cup) crunchy peanut butter

60 ml (¼ cup) lime juice

2 tablespoons soy sauce

1 teaspoon finely diced red chilli

1 teaspoon grated ginger

Soak the vermicelli noodles in a bowl of boiling water for 10–15 minutes, until tender. Strain through a sieve and allow to cool.

Meanwhile, peel the jicama, papaya and carrot, then cut into long thin strips. Place in a mixing bowl with the coriander and mint. Add the cooled noodles and mix well.

In a small bowl, combine all the dressing ingredients, mixing well. Drizzle over the noodle mixture and mix together well.

In a small bowl or jug, combine all the dipping sauce ingredients. Add 80 ml (⅓ cup) cold water and mix together thoroughly. Transfer to a dipping bowl for serving.

Working with one wrapper at a time, soak the rice paper sheets in a bowl of warm water for 2 seconds. Shake off the excess water and place on a clean bench, with one of the corners pointing towards you. Place a small handful of the noodle mixture in the middle. Fold the bottom corner over the mixture, fold the sides in, then roll the rice paper up, into a roll.

Repeat with the remaining rice paper sheets and filling, until you have 10 rolls.

Using a sharp knife, cut each roll through the middle, on the diagonal. Arrange on a platter, by sitting them upright on the base of each roll.

Serve immediately, with the dipping sauce.

BEST IN: SUMMER

ALREADY VEGAN!

Jicama & mango tostadas

SERVES 4

Also known as Mexican yam bean, Mexican water chestnut and Mexican turnip, jicama is a crunchy, juicy and slightly sweet member of the tuber family that is generally eaten raw. It can be found in Asian and Mexican greengrocers, as well as specialty greengrocers. Its papery skin can actually be peeled off by hand, but using a chef's knife will give the best result. –VV

60 ml (¼ cup) tequila

75 g (2¾ oz/½ cup) currants

1 avocado

juice of ½ lemon

vegetable oil, for shallow-frying

8 corn tortillas

coriander (cilantro), to garnish

JICAMA & MANGO SALAD

1 large jicama, peeled and diced

1 small red bell pepper (capsicum), diced

1 small yellow bell pepper (capsicum), diced

1 small red onion, finely diced

1 small cucumber, deseeded and diced

1 small mango, finely diced

3 tablespoons chopped coriander (cilantro)

½ teaspoon cayenne pepper

½ teaspoon sweet paprika

½ teaspoon sea salt

juice of 1 lime

2 tablespoons olive oil

Start by making the salad. In a large bowl, toss together the jicama, bell peppers, onion, cucumber, mango and coriander. Add the spices, lime juice and olive oil. Combine gently, then cover and set aside for 30 minutes.

Meanwhile, pour the tequila into a small saucepan and bring to a simmer over medium heat. Add the currants and simmer for 2 minutes. Remove from the heat and allow to soak for 10 minutes. Drain in a sieve, reserving the tequila, and set aside.

Peel the avocado and mash in a bowl, using a fork. Stir in the lemon juice and season with a pinch of salt and freshly ground black pepper.

Fill a medium-sized saucepan with 3 cm (1¼ in) of vegetable oil and heat over medium–high heat.

When the oil is hot, fry the tortillas one at a time for 30–40 seconds, until golden brown. Remove using a slotted spoon and drain on paper towel.

To serve, place the cooled tortillas on a large serving board and evenly divide the salad among them. Top with the avocado and currants. Spoon the reserved tequila and any remaining salad dressing over the top. Garnish with coriander and serve immediately.

BEST IN: SUMMER & SPRING

ALREADY VEGAN!

Bulbs
& Fungi

Asian mushrooms

button mushrooms

garlic

leeks

onions

porcini mushrooms

shallots

Swiss brown mushrooms

Mixed Asian mushroom stir-fry on a crisp noodle nest

SERVES 4

The combination of so many uniquely flavoured mushrooms makes for a beautiful dish. The varieties in this recipe can be found in some supermarkets and Asian greengrocers. If you are unable to locate a specific kind of mushroom, substitute it with one that is more readily available, preferably an Asian variety. –VV

3 dried Asian egg noodle nests

vegetable oil, for deep-frying

60 ml (¼ cup) sesame oil

100 g (3½ oz) shiitake mushrooms, cut in half

150 g (5½ oz) oyster mushrooms, separated

400 g (14 oz) pearl mushrooms (see Note), separated

300 g (10½ oz) shimeji mushrooms, separated

80 ml (⅓ cup) tamari

2 tablespoons finely grated ginger

4 garlic cloves, crushed

3 tablespoons chopped garlic chives

3 tablespoons chopped onion flowers or spring (green) onions

shredded spring (green) onions, to garnish

Half-fill a small saucepan with water and place over high heat. Bring to the boil and add the noodle nests. Cook according to the packet instructions, then drain in a colander.

Pour 4 cm (1½ in) of vegetable oil into a large saucepan. Place over high heat and bring to 180°C (350°F) on a cooking thermometer.

Using tongs, gently and carefully transfer the noodles to the hot oil, bit by bit, taking care the oil doesn't spill over. Fry for 6–8 minutes, until crisp; you will end up with one big noodle disc.

Using tongs, remove the noodle disc from the oil and place on paper towel to dry. Transfer to a serving dish.

Place a wok over high heat and add the sesame oil. Swirl the oil around the wok for 1 minute, or until smoking, then add all the mushrooms and toss for 3 minutes.

Add the tamari, ginger, garlic, garlic chives and onion flowers and toss for a further 2 minutes.

Pile the mixture on top of the crisp noodle disc. Garnish with spring onion and serve immediately.

BEST IN: AUTUMN

NOTE: Pearl mushrooms, or baby oyster mushrooms, are pale white or creamy toned in colour. They have long bodies with a slightly rounded mushroom head, and grow in clusters that are gently pulled apart into smaller clusters to cook.

Mushroom & ricotta ravioli with a lemon cream sauce

MAKES ABOUT 28 RAVIOLI

Taking the time to make pasta from scratch is such a satisfying experience. For best results, you'll really need to use a pasta machine for this one. If you don't have a pasta machine, beg steal or borrow one from a foodie friend or relative, invite them over and make an afternoon of it.

Don't forgo the porcini mushroom in this recipe – although it is only used in such a small quantity, it really adds a decadent flavour note. –VV

50 g (1¾ oz) unsalted butter

1 shallot, finely chopped

1 garlic clove, crushed

1 tablespoon lemon zest, plus extra to garnish

1 teaspoon finely chopped parsley

125 ml (½ cup) dry white wine

180 ml (¾ cup) thick (double/heavy) cream

shaved parmesan, to serve

parsley, to garnish

RAVIOLI DOUGH

600 g (1 lb 5 oz) '00' pasta flour (see Note on page 216), plus extra for dusting

6 free-range eggs, beaten

To make the dough, sift the flour into a large bowl and make a well in the centre. Pour in the egg and 2 tablespoons water. Using your hands, gently combine until a dough forms.

Turn the dough out onto a lightly floured surface and knead for 8 minutes, or until the dough is smooth and free of lumps. Wrap in plastic wrap and leave to rest at room temperature for 40 minutes.

Meanwhile, make the filling. Heat the olive oil in a frying pan, add the mushrooms, onion and garlic and sauté over medium heat for 6–7 minutes, stirring occasionally. Remove from the heat and stir in the parsley, ricotta and breadcrumbs. Season with salt and freshly ground black pepper and set aside to cool completely.

Cut the rested dough into eight portions. Using a pasta machine, roll out the dough, starting from the thickest setting, through to the thinnest. Place the pasta sheets on a lightly floured bench and cover with clean tea towels.

Uncover one sheet of dough. Place a teaspoon of filling on the top left-hand corner, at least 4 cm (1½ in) from the top and side edge. Continue placing more spoonfuls of the filling across the top of the sheet, leaving a 7 cm (2¾ in) gap between each.

Working across the bottom of the sheet, add more small mounds of filling, spacing them in between the top mounds, in a kind of zig-zag pattern.

MUSHROOM & RICOTTA FILLING

1 tablespoon olive oil

1 small dried porcini mushroom, rehydrated in water for 20 minutes, then finely diced

180 g (6½ oz) Swiss brown mushrooms, finely diced

1 small brown onion, finely diced

3 garlic cloves, crushed

1 tablespoon finely chopped parsley,

160 g (5½ oz/⅔ cup) fresh ricotta

2 tablespoons fine dry breadcrumbs

Using a pastry brush, moisten the pasta around the mounds with water.

Drape another pasta sheet on top. Gently press around the mushroom mounds to seal the pasta together. Using a 6 cm (2½ in) cookie cutter, cut out around each mound, and place each ravioli on a lightly floured tray.

Continue making more ravioli parcels with the remaining pasta sheets and filling. Set aside.

In a frying pan, melt the butter over low heat. Add the shallot and garlic and sauté for 3 minutes, or until translucent. Stir in the lemon zest and parsley, increase the heat to high and pour in the wine. Boil for 1 minute, then stir in the cream and allow to boil away for a further 2–3 minutes. Now reduce the heat and allow to simmer for a further 5–6 minutes, until the sauce is thick. Season with salt and pepper. Remove from the heat and cover to keep warm.

Bring a large saucepan of salted water to the boil. Add the ravioli and cook for 4–5 minutes, or until they float to the surface. Remove with a slotted spoon.

Drizzle half the warm cream sauce onto a platter and arrange the ravioli on top. Drizzle the remaining sauce over the top.

Serve immediately, garnished with shaved parmesan, parsley and some extra lemon zest.

BEST IN: AUTUMN

Mushroom & water chestnut pot stickers

MAKES 24

Try to stop at three or four of these tasty morsels! The filling is delightfully mushroomy and the water chestnuts add delicious crunch, all encased in a pleasingly chewy pastry with a crispy bottom. Gow gee wrappers are available from the refrigerator section of Asian grocery stores – most brands are vegan, but check the ingredients as some may contain egg. –CG

1 tablespoon peanut oil, plus extra for cooking the dumplings

75 g (2¾ oz/1 cup) shredded white cabbage

100 g (3½ oz) button mushrooms, chopped

50 g (1¾ oz) shiitake mushrooms (about 4), stems removed, chopped

1 garlic clove, crushed

1 free-range egg white

1 spring (green) onion, chopped

½ teaspoon finely grated ginger

½ teaspoon sesame oil

100 g (3½ oz) tinned or thawed frozen water chestnuts, sliced

24 round gow gee wrappers

BLACK VINEGAR DIPPING SAUCE

1 spring (green) onion, finely sliced

1 tablespoon Chinkiang vinegar (Chinese black vinegar)

1 tablespoon sesame oil

1 tablespoon soy sauce

1 teaspoon grated palm sugar

1 garlic clove, crushed

freshly ground white pepper, to taste

MAKE IT VEGAN!
Leave out the
egg white.

For the dipping sauce, put the spring onion, vinegar, sesame oil, soy sauce, sugar and garlic in a jar. Add 1 tablespoon water, seal the lid and shake until emulsified. Season to taste with a little white pepper. Set aside.

Heat the peanut oil in a non-stick frying pan over medium heat. Add the cabbage, mushrooms and garlic and cook, stirring, for 5–6 minutes, until tender. Remove from the heat, transfer to a bowl and set aside to cool.

Put half the cooled mushroom mixture in a food processor. Add the egg white, spring onion, ginger and sesame oil and whiz until finely chopped. Return to the remaining mixture with the water chestnuts and mix well.

Working in batches, place the gow gee wrappers on a clean surface. Place 2 teaspoons of the mushroom mixture in the centre of each wrapper. Using your finger, brush the wrapper edges lightly with water. Fold one side of the wrapper over and pleat and pinch the edges to seal. This will help to give the dumpling its classic curved shape. Place on a tray and cover with plastic wrap to stop the dumplings drying out as you go. (The dumplings can be made 2–3 hours ahead; refrigerate until ready to use.)

Heat 2 teaspoons of peanut oil in a large non-stick frying pan with a lid over medium heat. When the pan is hot, add half the dumplings, seam-side up, in a single layer. Pour in 125 ml (½ cup) water, cover with a tight-fitting lid and steam for 5 minutes.

Remove the lid and cook the dumplings for a further 4–5 minutes, or until the water has evaporated and the dumplings release from the pan, and are golden and crunchy on the bottom. Transfer to a plate and cover loosely with foil to keep warm.

Heat another 2 teaspoons peanut oil in the pan. Cook the remaining dumplings in the same way, adding another 125 ml (½ cup) water to the pan.

Serve the dumplings warm, with the dipping sauce.

BEST: ALL YEAR ROUND

Mushroom pot pie with a creamy kohlrabi & kale mash

MAKES 4 × 500 ML (2 CUP) RAMEKINS, OR 1 LARGE POT PIE

A lovely winter warmer, suitable for serving individually, or as a main pie dish with crusty fresh bread and a glass of red wine. This mash also works beautifully as a side dish, or even in place of the smoky polenta in the recipe on page 54. –VV

20 g (¾ oz) butter

800 g (1 lb 12 oz) white cup mushrooms, sliced

800 g (1 lb 12 oz) large flat Swiss brown mushrooms, sliced

1 small leek, white part only, sliced

2 garlic cloves, finely sliced

1 tablespoon fresh thyme leaves

2 tablespoons plain (all-purpose) flour

100 ml (3½ fl oz) dry white wine

200 ml (7 fl oz) thickened (whipping) cream (35% fat)

KOHLRABI & KALE MASH

500 g (1 lb 2 oz) kohlrabi, peeled and diced

500 g (1 lb 2 oz) potatoes, peeled and diced

45 g (1½ oz/1½ cups) chopped Tuscan kale (cavolo nero)

60 g (2 oz) butter

2 garlic cloves, crushed

60 ml (¼ cup) thickened (whipping) cream (35% fat)

50 g (1¾ oz/½ cup) grated parmesan

Preheat the oven to 180°C/350°F (fan-forced).

Melt the butter in a large frying pan over medium heat. Add the mushrooms and leek and sauté for 6–8 minutes, or until softened.

Stir in the garlic and thyme, followed by the flour. Continue stirring for 1 minute, then pour in the wine, cream and 125 ml (½ cup) water, stirring until smooth. Reduce the heat and simmer for 10 minutes, or until the mixture is thick and coats the back of a spoon. Set aside.

For the mash, bring a saucepan of water to the boil and add the kohlrabi, potato and kale. Cook for 10 minutes, or until the vegetables are tender.

Drain the vegetables in a colander, then return to the pan. Stir in the butter, garlic, cream and parmesan. Using a hand-held stick blender, purée the mixture to a medium consistency, leaving a few lumps here and there.

Season the mushroom mixture with salt and freshly ground black pepper. Spoon into four individual 500 ml (2 cup) ramekins, or a 2 litre (8 cup) pie dish, leaving 2 cm (¾ in) free at the top for the mash topping.

Spoon the mash mixture over the top of the mushroom mixture. Use the back of the spoon to evenly spread the mash to the top of the ramekin line. If there is any mash remaining, add a few heaped spoonfuls here and there on top.

Place the ramekins on a baking tray and bake for 20–25 minutes for the smaller ramekins, or 40–55 minutes for the large pie, until the mash is golden brown.

Remove from the oven and leave to settle for 5 minutes before serving.

BEST IN: AUTUMN & WINTER

Mushroom & chestnut soup with truffled chestnuts & crème fraîche

SERVES 4

Vacuum-packed chestnuts can be found in delicatessens and specialty food stores. They are a great alternative for a less involved preparation of this recipe, and for those of us who are a little time poor. Truffled chestnuts, which you will also find in specialty delicatessens, are the perfect garnish for impressing dinner guests. –VV

2 tablespoons olive oil

1 large brown onion, chopped

1 shallot, finely chopped

1 garlic clove, crushed

2 dried porcini mushrooms, rehydrated in water for 20 minutes, then chopped

150 g (5½ oz) button mushrooms

1 small parsnip, peeled and chopped

1 small apple, peeled, cored and chopped

200 g (7 oz) vacuum-packed chestnuts, chopped

4 thyme sprigs

1.25 litres (5 cups) Vegetable stock (see page 23)

1 teaspoon sea salt

½ teaspoon freshly ground black pepper

crème fraîche, to serve

thinly sliced truffled chestnuts, to garnish

crushed pink peppercorns, to garnish

Pour the olive oil into a large saucepan over high heat. Add the onion, shallot and garlic and sauté for 3 minutes. Add the mushrooms, parsnip, apple, chestnuts and thyme sprigs, stirring them through thoroughly. Reduce the heat to medium, then cover and cook for 8 minutes.

Remove the lid and increase the heat to high. Ladle in all the vegetable stock. Bring to the boil, then reduce the heat to a simmer and cook for a further 25 minutes. Remove from the heat and leave to cool slightly.

Using a hand-held stick blender, carefully purée the mixture until smooth. Stir in the salt and pepper and gently reheat until warmed through.

Ladle into warm bowls and serve immediately, topped with crème fraîche, truffled chestnut slices and a sprinkling of crushed pink peppercorns.

BEST IN: AUTUMN & WINTER

Mushroom, tomato & barley 'risotto'

SERVES 4

Using barley rather than rice to make a risotto-style dish makes an interesting change. It is hearty, textural, warming and full of flavour. –CG

2 tablespoons dried porcini mushrooms

300 g (10½ oz) Swiss brown mushrooms

20 g (¾ oz) butter

1 tablespoon olive oil

1 onion, chopped

1 carrot, chopped

1 celery stalk, chopped

2 garlic cloves, crushed

1 teaspoon finely chopped rosemary

1 litre (4 cups) Vegetable stock (see page 23)

400 g (14 oz) tin chopped tomatoes

220 g (8 oz/1 cup) pearl barley, rinsed

50 g (1¾ oz/½ cup) grated parmesan, plus extra to serve

handful of parsley, chopped, plus extra to garnish

MAKE IT VEGAN!
Replace the butter with olive oil and substitute a few teaspoons of nutritional yeast for the grated parmesan.

Put the dried porcini mushrooms in a small bowl and cover with warm water. Soak for 15 minutes, then strain the mushrooms, reserving the liquid and discarding any grit from the sieve.

Roughly chop the porcini. Slice and chop the fresh mushrooms so that there is some variation in size and appearance between them. Set aside.

Heat the butter and olive oil in a large heavy-based saucepan over low–medium heat. Add the onion, carrot, celery, garlic and rosemary and cook, stirring occasionally, for 10 minutes, or until soft. Add the fresh mushrooms and soaked porcini and sauté for 8 minutes, or until softened. Remove about ½ cup of the mushroom mixture and set aside for serving.

Pour in the stock and reserved porcini soaking water. Stir in the tomatoes and barley and bring to the boil. Reduce the heat to low and cook, stirring occasionally, for 40 minutes, or until the barley is tender. Add a little boiling water along the way if you feel more moisture is required.

Stir in the parmesan. Cover and set aside to rest for 5 minutes.

Stir in the parsley and serve, topped with the reserved mushroom mixture and some extra parsley and parmesan.

BEST IN: AUTUMN, WINTER & SPRING

Onion tarte tatin

SERVES 8

You can use a combination of baby onions and shallots for this tart, or just make it with your favourite member of the allium family. If some of your baby onions are slightly larger, cut them in half and place them cut side down in the pan, just before you top them with the pastry – they'll look good too, like little onion flowers. –CG

800 g (1 lb 12 oz) shallots and/or baby onions, unpeeled

50 g (1¾ oz) butter

2 tablespoons olive oil (or use the oil from the Garlic confit on page 245)

2 tablespoons rapadura sugar or brown sugar

2 thyme sprigs, leaves picked, plus extra to garnish

60 ml (¼ cup) red wine vinegar

8–10 Confit garlic cloves (see page 245)

flour, for dusting

350 g (12½ oz) block of frozen good-quality puff pastry, or 2 puff pastry sheets, thawed

MAKE IT VEGAN!
Replace the butter with a non-dairy alternative or use more olive oil. Check the pastry packaging to ensure vegan ingredients are used.

Put the shallots and/or baby onions in a heatproof bowl and pour over enough boiling water to cover them. Leave for 10 minutes, or until cool enough to handle, then drain and peel.

Preheat the oven to 180°C/350°F (fan-forced).

In a 20–22 cm (8–8¾ in) heavy-based ovenproof frying pan or tarte tatin pan, heat the butter and olive oil over low heat. Add the peeled bulbs and cook gently for 15–20 minutes, or until quite soft and lightly browned.

Stir in the sugar, thyme leaves and vinegar. Season with salt and freshly ground black pepper. Cook for a further 5–6 minutes, or until the liquid has reduced and caramelised. Remove from the heat and set aside to cool for 10 minutes.

Nestle the cloves of garlic, evenly spaced, under the bulbs on the bottom of the pan. If any of the baby onions are a little larger than the rest, cut them in half horizontally and place them cut side down in the pan.

On a lightly floured surface, roll out the pastry to about 3 mm (⅒ in) thick and cut out a circle slightly larger than the pan. (If using pastry sheets, press them together and trim to a circle.) Prick the pastry all over with a fork and place it on top of the bulbs. Ease the edge of the pastry between the bulbs and the side of the pan.

Transfer the pan to the oven and bake for 30–35 minutes, or until the pastry is cooked through, puffed and a deep golden brown.

Remove from the oven and allow to settle for 10 minutes.

Place a large serving plate upside-down on top of the pan, then carefully turn the tart upside down onto the plate. Serve warm or cold, scattered with extra thyme.

BEST: ALL YEAR ROUND

Cashew & onion pilau

SERVES 6

The perfect side dish for Indian curries and dhal, serve this fragrant pilau alongside some naan breads, raita and spicy pickles to round off the perfect meal experience. –VV

2 tablespoons coconut oil

2 red onions, halved and finely sliced

2 teaspoons yellow mustard seeds

115 g (4 oz/¾ cup) raw cashews

45 g (1½ oz/½ cup) flaked almonds

30 g (1 oz/½ cup) shredded coconut

4 cardamom pods, crushed

1 cinnamon stick

1 teaspoon cumin seeds

4 whole cloves

1 tablespoon ground turmeric

2 dried bay leaves

8 fresh curry leaves

600 g (1 lb 5 oz/3 cups) basmati rice

1 teaspoon sea salt

75 g (2¾ oz/½ cup) currants

Melt the coconut oil in a frying pan over medium heat. Add the onion and sauté for 10 minutes, or until translucent. Transfer to a small bowl using a slotted spoon.

Add the mustard seeds, cashews, almonds and coconut to the same pan. Cook, stirring occasionally, for 3 minutes, or until the nuts and coconut are golden. Add the mixture to the sautéed onion.

Place the cardamom pods, cinnamon stick, cumin seeds, cloves, turmeric, bay leaves and curry leaves in a saucepan over high heat. Stir in the rice, salt, currants and 1 litre (4 cups) water. Bring to the boil, then reduce the heat to low. Cover and simmer for 10 minutes, or until the liquid has been absorbed.

Remove from the heat and leave to stand for 5 minutes.

Fold the sautéed onion and nuts through the rice mixture, mixing gently to combine. Serve immediately.

BEST IN: AUTUMN & WINTER

ALREADY VEGAN!

Onion soup with stilton toasts

SERVES 6

Classic onion soup is great in cooler seasons, either served as a starter or on its own as a main. The sharp and full-bodied flavour of stilton on the toasts pares back the sweetness of the onion soup superbly. –VV

60 ml (¼ cup) olive oil

4 large white onions, finely sliced

1 leek, white part only, finely sliced

3 celery stalks, chopped

5 garlic cloves, crushed

1 green chilli, deseeded and chopped

3 tablespoons chopped ginger

1 tablespoon mirin

125 ml (½ cup) dry white wine

3 small crusty baguettes, sliced in half lengthways

150 g (5½ oz/1 cup) crumbled stilton

GINGER-INFUSED STOCK

1 carrot, chopped

2 celery stalks, chopped

1 garlic clove

1 onion, skin on, cut in half

1 cm (½ in) piece of ginger

1 spring (green) onion, cut in half

½ teaspoon black peppercorns

1 teaspoon sea salt

Start by making the ginger-infused stock. Place all the ingredients in a large saucepan. Pour in 1.5 litres (6 cups) water and bring to the boil over high heat. Reduce the heat, then cover and simmer for 1 hour.

Pass through a sieve, into a large bowl. Set aside.

Pour the olive oil into a large saucepan over medium heat. Add the onion, leek, celery, garlic, chilli and ginger and sauté for 10 minutes, or until translucent.

Increase the heat to high and stir in the mirin and wine. Ladle in all the stock and bring back to the boil, then reduce the heat and simmer for 30 minutes. Remove from the heat and allow to cool.

Using a hand-held stick blender, purée the soup until smooth and free of lumps. Season with salt and freshly ground black pepper and gently reheat for serving.

Meanwhile, heat the grill (broiler) to medium. Place the baguette slices on the grill tray, cut side up, and sprinkle with the stilton. Toast under the grill for 3–4 minutes, or until the cheese has melted.

Ladle the soup into warm bowls and serve immediately, with the stilton toasts.

BEST IN: AUTUMN & WINTER

Grilled leeks with agrodolce

SERVES 4

Use baby leeks if you are lucky enough to find them, otherwise small leeks work very well too, but will take a little longer to cook. It is really important to wash leeks well, as grit loves to lurk between the layers, especially where the leek starts to turn darker green.

Agrodolce, a classic sauce with a special balance of sour and sweet flavours, is wonderful with the soft silkiness of the grilled leeks. –CG

12 baby leeks or 4 small leeks

olive oil, for drizzling

AGRODOLCE

1 tablespoon raisins

1 tablespoon dried sour cherries

1 small red chilli, finely sliced

90 g (3 oz/¼ cup) honey

125 ml (½ cup) red wine vinegar

sea salt flakes, to taste

2 tablespoons pine nuts, toasted

MAKE IT VEGAN!
Replace the honey
with 2–3 tablespoons
of agave syrup.

Trim the baby leeks to get rid of any outer tough layers, or if using small leeks trim them down just past the tough dark green leaves. Cut the smaller leeks in half lengthways. Wash well in cold water to release any grit from between the layers, then pat dry with paper towel or a clean tea towel.

Heat a chargrill pan or barbecue grill to high heat. Drizzle the leeks with a little olive oil. Chargrill the baby leeks whole, or the halved leeks with the cut side down first. Char for 4–5 minutes, until well marked and lightly browned all over. Transfer to a shallow roasting tin.

Preheat the oven to 160°C/320°F (fan-forced).

For the agrodolce, put the raisins, cherries, chilli, honey and vinegar in a small saucepan and add a good pinch of sea salt flakes. Bring to the boil over medium heat, then reduce the heat to a simmer and cook for 10–15 minutes, until slightly thickened and syrupy. Stir in the pine nuts.

Spoon about half the agrodolce mixture over the leeks. If using small leeks, cover the roasting tin with foil.

Transfer the leeks to the oven. Bake the baby leeks for 12–15 minutes, or the small leeks for 15–20 minutes, until very tender.

Spoon the remaining agrodolce over the warm leeks and serve.

BEST IN: AUTUMN, WINTER & SPRING

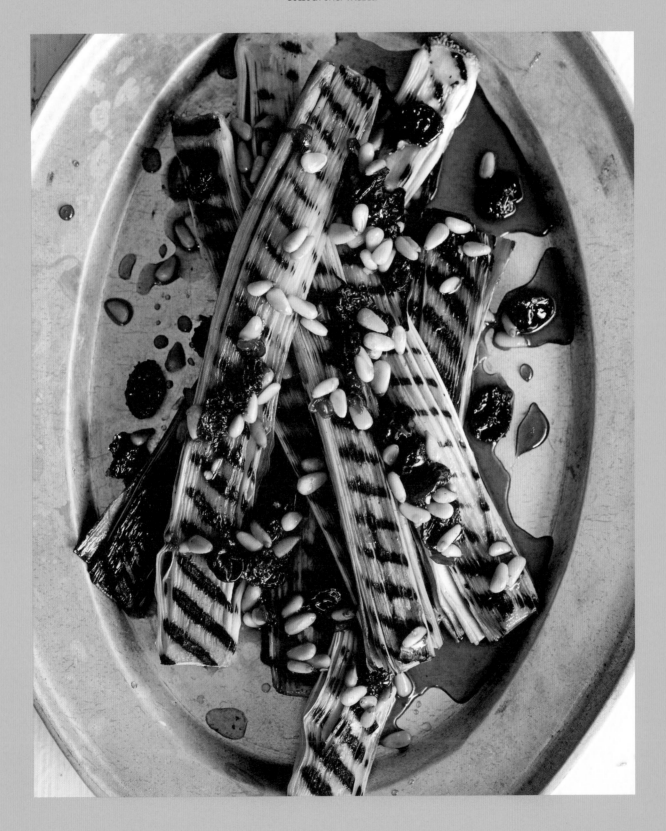

Leek & potato soup

SERVES 4

This soup is one of those go-to comfort foods. Develop a depth of flavour by browning the potatoes lightly in the saucepan before adding the stock. You can leave this soup with a little texture or, if you prefer, blend until silky smooth. If you are after a quick soup, leave off the fancy topping. –CG

2 leeks

800 g (1 lb 12 oz) all-purpose potatoes

20 g (¾ oz) butter

1 tablespoon olive oil, plus extra for
shallow-frying

750 ml (3 cups) Vegetable stock
(see page 23)

80 ml (⅓ cup) pouring (single/light)
cream, plus extra for drizzling (optional)

MAKE IT VEGAN!
Use olive oil instead
of butter, leave out the
cream and add a splash
of oat milk instead.

Trim the leeks, leaving only the white and pale green parts, discarding the tough green leaves. Cut a 10 cm (4 in) length from the greener end of one leek, rinse and set it aside for the topping. Cut the leeks in half lengthways and soak in plenty of cold water to remove any dirt. Finely slice and set aside.

Set one of the potatoes aside, unpeeled, for the topping, after giving it a good scrub. Peel the remaining potatoes, chop into chunks and set aside.

Heat the butter and olive oil in a large heavy-based saucepan over medium heat. Add the sliced leek and cook for 10 minutes, or until softened.

Add the chopped potato, stir well and cook for a further 5 minutes, stirring occasionally, until the potato starts to take on some colour and sticks to the base of the pan slightly. Pour in the stock. It should just cover the vegetables; if not, add a little water to top it up. Bring to the boil, then reduce the heat to a simmer. Cover and cook for 15–20 minutes, until the potato is very tender.

Meanwhile, in a small saucepan, heat about 2 cm (¾ in) of olive oil over medium heat, until it reaches 180°C (350°F) on a cooking thermometer, or a cube of bread dropped into the oil turns golden in 15 seconds.

Slice the reserved green of the leek into long thin strips. Deep-fry the leek strips in batches for about 30 seconds, until crisp and golden. Remove with a slotted spoon and drain on paper towel.

Using a potato peeler, and working in batches, peel strips of the reserved potato straight into the oil. Deep-fry the potato strips for 2–3 minutes, until crisp. Drain on paper towel and season with a little salt.

Using a hand-held stick blender, purée the soup until smooth. Stir in the cream, if using, and season with salt and freshly ground black pepper.

Ladle the soup into warm bowls. Serve with an extra drizzle of cream, if desired, and top with the crispy potato and leek strips.

BEST IN: AUTUMN, WINTER & SPRING

Pickled shallots

MAKES 2 × 400 ML (13½ FL OZ) JARS

These pickled shallots are great served on a ploughman's board along with some sharp cheese, cornichons, caperberries, quince paste and crusty bread. Another favourite is to serve them finely sliced on fresh bread, topped with cheddar and toasted. –VV

1½ tablespoons coriander seeds

1 tablespoon yellow mustard seeds

5 whole cloves

1 tablespoon pink peppercorns

1 tablespoon black peppercorns

500 ml (2 cups) white wine vinegar

½ teaspoon chilli flakes

70 g (2½ oz/⅓ cup) brown sugar

2 dried bay leaves

500 g (1 lb 2 oz) shallots, peeled

ALREADY VEGAN!

Preheat the oven to 180°C/350°F (fan-forced). Wash two 400 ml (13½ fl oz) jars and lids with warm soapy water, rinse well and place in the oven for 30 minutes to sterilise them.

Remove the jars and lids from the oven and leave until cool enough to handle.

Meanwhile, place the coriander seeds, mustard seeds, cloves and pink and black peppercorns in a saucepan over medium heat. Toss for 1 minute, or until fragrant.

Pour in the vinegar and 250 ml (1 cup) water. Add the chilli flakes, sugar and bay leaves. Bring to the boil for 3 minutes, then reduce the heat to medium and add the shallots. Simmer for 8–10 minutes, or until the shallots are just tender when pierced with a skewer.

Using a slotted spoon, divide the shallots between the jars. Ladle in the pickling juice, including the spices, filling the jars to the top.

Seal, label and place in a cool dark place for 5 days before eating.

The pickles will keep in the pantry for 12 months. Once opened, store in the fridge and use within 4 weeks.

BEST IN: AUTUMN & WINTER

Roasted garlic soup with parmesan paprika croutons

SERVES 4

Roasted garlic has a sweeter and milder flavour than garlic in its raw state. Some specialty greengrocers also stock smoked garlic – this works well in this recipe and is highly recommended if you are looking to introduce an even richer flavour. –VV

60 g (2 oz) unsalted butter

1 brown onion, sliced

1 teaspoon chopped thyme

15 garlic cloves, peeled

2 dried bay leaves

1 litre (4 cups) Vegetable stock (see page 23)

125 ml (½ cup) thick (double/heavy) cream

ROASTED GARLIC

2 whole garlic bulbs, sliced in half horizontally

2 tablespoons olive oil

PARMESAN PAPRIKA CROUTONS

60 g (2 oz) unsalted butter

1 tablespoon crushed fresh garlic

½ teaspoon smoked paprika

6 slices sourdough bread, cut into 2 cm (¾ inch) chunks

50 g (1¾ oz/½ cup) grated parmesan

To roast the garlic, preheat the oven to 160°C/320°F (fan-forced). Place the garlic bulb halves on a baking tray, drizzle with the olive oil and season with salt. Cover with foil and bake for 30 minutes, or until the garlic has browned.

Remove from the oven and leave to cool completely. Squeeze the roasted garlic out of their skins into a small bowl. Set aside.

Melt the butter in a large saucepan over medium heat. Add the onion, thyme, whole garlic cloves and bay leaves and sauté for 2 minutes. Ladle in the vegetable stock, then stir in the roasted garlic. Cover and simmer for 30 minutes, or until the garlic cloves are tender.

Remove from the heat, stir in the cream and allow to cool completely. Transfer to a blender and whiz to a smooth purée. Season with salt and freshly ground black pepper and gently reheat for serving.

Meanwhile, preheat the oven to 180°C/350°F (fan-forced) and prepare the croutons. Melt the butter in a large saucepan over medium heat. Stir in the garlic and paprika until well combined, then add the bread cubes and toss until thoroughly coated.

Transfer the bread cubes to a lined baking tray and sprinkle with the parmesan. Bake for 10 minutes, or until the cheese is golden.

Ladle the soup into warm bowls and serve immediately, topped with the sourdough croutons.

BEST IN: SPRING & SUMMER

Onion bhajis

MAKES ABOUT 35

The combination of chickpea flour and rice flour gives these bhajis, with their crispy spidery legs, an addictive texture. I like to use a combination of brown and red onion, but any will do. –CG

1 brown onion, halved and finely sliced

1 red onion, halved and finely sliced

1 small red chilli, chopped, plus extra to garnish

1 teaspoon ground turmeric, plus extra to garnish

1 teaspoon grated ginger

2 garlic cloves, crushed

½ teaspoon salt

1 teaspoon cumin seeds

1 tablespoon lemon juice

70 g (2½ oz/½ cup) besan (chickpea) flour

50 g (1¾ oz/¼ cup) brown rice flour

1½ teaspoons baking powder

peanut oil, for deep-frying

plain vegan yoghurt, to serve

Put the onions in a mixing bowl. Add the chilli, turmeric, ginger, garlic and salt. Using one hand, massage the onion mixture for 1–2 minutes, until the onion starts to soften and the juices start to run from the onion. Stir in the cumin seeds and lemon juice.

Sift the flours and baking powder over the onion mixture and mix well until combined. Add about 60 ml (¼ cup) water to the mixture to make a smooth batter that coats the onion. Stir in a little more water, if necessary – the mixture should not be thick.

Fill a wok or deep wide medium–small saucepan no more than one-third full with peanut oil. Heat the oil until it reaches 180°C (350°F) on a cooking thermometer, or a cube of bread dropped into the oil turns golden in 15 seconds.

Working in batches, add heaped teaspoons of the onion mixture to the oil and cook for 3–4 minutes, or until the batter is a deep golden colour and cooked through. Remove with a slotted spoon and drain on paper towel while cooking the remaining bhajis.

Serve warm with yoghurt, sprinkled with a little extra turmeric and chopped chilli.

BEST IN: AUTUMN & WINTER

ALREADY VEGAN!

Garlic confit with warm flatbreads

MAKES ABOUT 1 CUP GARLIC CLOVES IN OIL

Fresh, locally grown garlic is ideal for this magical condiment, but any good-quality garlic will do. Not only will you have meltingly soft and savoury garlic to add to all kinds of dishes – such as the Onion tarte tatin on page 233 – you'll also have a deliciously subtle garlic oil for cooking, drizzling or to use in salad dressings. Just ensure that you keep your confit in the fridge or freezer, not at room temperature, so it stays food safe. –CG

3 garlic bulbs, cloves peeled

180 ml (¾ cup) olive oil, approximately

1 quantity Quick flatbread dough (see page 108)

Put the garlic in a small heavy-based saucepan and pour over enough olive oil to just cover the garlic.

Warm the mixture over medium heat until bubbles just start to rise to the surface. Reduce the heat to very low. Using a heat diffuser if necessary, very gently poach (don't boil or fry) the garlic cloves for 40–45 minutes, or until tender and very lightly browned. Remove from the heat and cool to room temperature.

Meanwhile, preheat the oven to 180°C/350°F (fan-forced). Wash a 300 ml (10 fl oz) jar and lid with warm soapy water, rinse well and place in the oven for 30 minutes to sterilise them.

Remove the jar and lid from the oven and set aside until cool enough to handle.

Spoon the garlic cloves into the sterilised jar, then cover with the poaching oil. Seal and label the jar, then move to the refrigerator, where the confit will keep for up to 3 weeks. (Alternatively, it will keep in an airtight container in the freezer for up to 2 months.)

When ready to serve, prepare the flatbreads according to the recipe on page 108, but rolling the dough into ovals measuring about 20 cm × 10 cm (8 in × 4 in). Brush with a little garlic oil from the confit before cooking.

Serve the garlic confit at room temperature, with the warm flatbreads, and a little extra garlic oil to drizzle if you like.

BEST IN: SUMMER

Index

A

agrodolce 236
aioli
    Truffle aioli 125
amaranth
    Amaranth with soba noodles & black sesame
        dressing 52
    Spanakopita 51
Ann's potato, cheese & onion pie 200
Aquafaba mayo 184
artichoke hearts
    Artichoke, basil & baby pea lasagne 24
artichoke, globe
    Braised broad beans with artichoke, peas &
        dill 79
    Fresh artichoke salad with lemon, celery &
        herbs 14
    Sumac chickpea salad with fennel &
        artichoke 22
Asian gazpacho 96
asparagus
    Asparagus & fennel galette with goat's
        cheese 26
    Butter-poached asparagus with salt-cured
        egg yolks 17
    Charred asparagus & broccolini with garlic
        olive crumbs 18
avocado
    Avocado & corn salsa 68
    Avocado dressing 102
    Spicy avocado & watermelon salad with mint &
        jalapeño chilli 113

B

Baba ghanoush & tomato salad with quick
    flatbreads 108
Banana blossom & green papaya salad 31
barley
    Mushroom, tomato & barley 'risotto' 231
basil
    Artichoke, basil & baby pea lasagne 24
    Basil emulsion 92
    Basil oil 77
    Ricotta-stuffed zucchini flowers 12
    Squash with lemon & basil 120
BBQ corn with chipotle mayo & queso fresco 80
beans, green
    Green bean & burghul salad with currants &
        crisp-fried capers 66
    Green bean salad with grilled haloumi &
        rum-soaked figs 73
    Snake bean, vegetable & tofu curry 64

    Steamed beans with lemon &
        pistachio dukkah 67
    Wax beans with candied walnuts & feta 70
    Zucchini, mango & green bean salad 126
Bean sprouts stir-fry in egg net 86
beetroot
    Beetroot & carrot casserole 175
    Raw beetroot relish with sesame 185
bell peppers
    Panzanella 92
    Rainbow slaw with avocado dressing 102
    Red pepper rouille on kipflers with toasted
        walnuts 98
Biryani-stuffed pumpkins 134
Black bean & jalapeño fritters with avocado &
    corn salsa 68
black rice
    Cabbage rolls stuffed with black rice &
        raisins 165
    Spanakorizo 49
Black sesame dressing 52
Black vinegar dipping sauce 226
black-eyed peas
    Mexican zucchini, peas & corn salad 122
bok choy
    Rainbow slaw with avocado dressing 102
    Salad of pea shoots & watercress with soy
        eggs 32
Braised broad beans with artichoke,
    peas & dill 79
Braised celery with blue cheese 15
Braised lettuce with broad beans & peas 45
Braised silverbeet & lentils 48
broad beans
    Braised broad beans with artichoke, peas &
        dill 79
    Braised lettuce with broad beans & peas 45
broccoli & broccolini
    Broccolini with poached eggs & miso
        hollandaise 147
    Carrot, cauliflower, broccoli & mustard
        gratin 174
    Charred asparagus & broccolini with garlic olive
        crumbs 18
    Orzo salad with kale, broccoli & lemon 144
    Roasted broccolini, kale & chickpeas with
        herbed ricotta 143
brussels sprouts
    Roasted maple sprouts with pecans 167
    Shaved brussels sprouts & freekeh salad 162
burghul
    Green bean & burghul salad with currants &
        crisp-fried capers 66

burrata
    Watercress salad with burrata 46

C

cabbage
    Cabbage rolls stuffed with black rice &
        raisins 165
    Eggplant schnitzels with buttermilk slaw 104
    Kimchi with turmeric 156
    Okonomiyaki 161
    Rainbow slaw with avocado dressing 102
    Raw kohlrabi & cabbage salad with peanut, lime
        & sesame dressing 164
cannellini beans
    Pea & cannellini bean mash with basil oil 77
    Ultra-greens soup 41
capers
    Green bean & burghul salad with currants &
        crisp-fried capers 66
carrots
    Beetroot & carrot casserole 175
    Carrot, cauliflower, broccoli & mustard
        gratin 174
    Roasted carrot soup with coriander & mint
        pesto 172
    Spiced roasted baby carrot salad with kaffir
        coconut dressing 177
cashews
    Cashew & onion pilau 234
    Steamed choy sum with sesame cashews 34
cauliflower
    Carrot, cauliflower, broccoli & mustard
        gratin 174
    Cauliflower 'steaks' with tahini & mint
        dressing 152
    Cauliflower 'tabbouleh' salad 150
    Roast cauliflower with pomegranate &
        yoghurt 148
    Three-way cauliflower soup 151
celeriac
    Celeriac, brown onion & mustard tart 187
    Celeriac & lemon mash with mustard &
        buttermilk 182
    Celeriac & rocket remoulade with aquafaba
        mayo 184
    Sweet potato & celeriac bake 208
celery
    Braised celery with blue cheese 15
    Fresh artichoke salad with lemon, celery &
        herbs 14
    removing 'strings' 15
    Shaved fennel salad with citrus 28

Charred asparagus & broccolini with garlic olive crumbs 18
Charred baby cos with salsa verde 42
Charred tomatillo tostadas 95
cheese
  Ann's potato, cheese & onion pie 200
  Asparagus & fennel galette with goat's cheese 26
  BBQ corn with chipotle mayo & queso fresco 80
  Braised celery with blue cheese 15
  parmesan rinds 40
  Potato, cheddar & jalapeño croquettes 202
  Ricotta-stuffed zucchini flowers 12
  Roasted garlic soup with parmesan paprika croutons 241
  Smoky polenta with garlic & silverbeet 54
  Zucchini, mint & cheese fritters 116
  see also burrata; feta; goat's cheese; haloumi; ricotta; stilton
chestnuts
  Mushroom & chestnut soup with truffled chestnuts & crème fraîche 230
  truffled 230
  vacuum-packed 230
chickpeas
  Roasted broccolini, kale & chickpeas with herbed ricotta 143
  Sumac chickpea salad with fennel & artichoke 22
chilli
  Banana blossom & green papaya salad 31
  Lime, chilli & shoyu dressing 217
  Spicy avocado & watermelon salad with mint & jalapeño chilli 113
chipotle
  Chipotle mayo 81
  Roasted eggplant with chipotle & lime 103
choy sum
  Steamed choy sum with sesame cashews 34
chutney
  Indian-style tomato chutney 97
  Spiced rhubarb chutney 35
citrus fruit
  segmenting 28
  Shaved fennel salad with citrus 28
  see also grapefruit; lemon; lime; orange
coconut
  Kaffir coconut dressing 177
  Spinach & green curry coconut soup 39
coriander
  Coriander & mint pesto 172
  Green sauce 206
  pickling vinegar 158
  Pistachio dukkah 67
  Zucchini, mint & cheese fritters 116
corn
  Avocado & corn salsa 68
  BBQ corn with chipotle mayo & queso fresco 80
  Corn tikkis with raita & tamarind sauce 83
  Mexican zucchini, peas & corn salad 122
  Sweet potato & corn empanadas 206
  Tempura baby corn with togarashi mayo 84
cranberries
  Grilled witlof with cranberry & pistachio 56
crème fraîche
  Fennel soup 23
  Mushroom & chestnut soup with truffled chestnuts & crème fraîche 230
Crispy potato stacks 199
Crostini 46
Crumbed zucchini batons with truffle aioli 125
cucumber
  Asian gazpacho 96
  Panzanella 92
  Sesame cucumber salad 130
  Sweet & sour cucumber 110
currants
  Green bean & burghul salad with currants & crisp-fried capers 66
curry
  Red curry pumpkin dip 139
  Snake bean, vegetable & tofu curry 64
  Spinach & green curry coconut soup 39

D

Daikon pickle 191
dhal
  Spicy pumpkin dhal 138
dill
  Braised broad beans with artichoke, peas & dill 79
  Dill fettuccine with Jerusalem artichoke 216
  Herbed ricotta 143
  Ricotta-stuffed zucchini flowers 12
dip
  Red curry pumpkin dip 139
dipping sauce
  Black vinegar dipping sauce 227
  Lime, ginger & peanut dipping sauce 217
dressings
  Avocado dressing 102
  Black sesame dressing 52
  Garlic vinegar dressing 22
  Garlic yoghurt dressing 137
  Kaffir coconut dressing 177
  Lemon mustard dressing 123
  Lemon vinaigrette 14
  Lemon yoghurt dressing 14
  Lime & cayenne dressing 122
  Lime & chilli dressing 126
  Lime, chilli & shoyu dressing 217
  Lime & garlic dressing 31
  Lime & sesame dressing 119
  Orange mustard dressing 46
  Orange & pomegranate dressing 162
  Peanut, lime & sesame dressing 164
  Red wine vinegar dressing 28
  Shiro miso dressing 106
  Tahini & mint dressing 152
dukkah
  nut-free 67
  Pistachio dukkah 67
  Roast turnips with goat's cheese & dukkah 190

E

edamame
  Lotus root, water chestnut & edamame stir-fry 181
  Okonomiyaki 161
  Smashed edamame with mint & soba noodles 74
egg noodles
  Mixed Asian mushroom stir-fry on a crisp noodle nest 223
eggs
  Bean sprouts stir-fry in egg net 86
  Broccolini with poached eggs & miso hollandaise 147
  Butter-poached asparagus with salt-cured egg yolks 17
  leftover yolks 17
  Salad of pea shoots & watercress with soy eggs 32
  Salt-cured egg yolks 17
  Soy eggs 32
eggplant
  Baba ghanoush & tomato salad with quick flatbreads 108
  Eggplant schnitzels with buttermilk slaw 104
  Miso eggplant & soba noodle salad 106
  Roasted eggplant with chipotle & lime 103
  Sichuan eggplant 107
empanadas
  Sweet potato & corn empanadas 206
endive
  Grilled witlof with cranberry & pistachio 56

F

fennel
  Asparagus & fennel galette with goat's cheese 26
  Fennel gratin 21
  Fennel soup 23
  Shaved fennel salad with citrus 28
  Sumac chickpea salad with fennel & artichoke 22
feta
  Filo cigars with nettles & hummus 60
  Kale, ricotta & feta rolls 154
  Roasted parsnips with hazelnuts & feta 171
  Shaved fennel salad with citrus 28
  Spanakopita 51
  Wax beans with candied walnuts & feta 70
  Whole baked sweet potatoes with lentils, feta & olives 211
  Zucchini, mint & cheese fritters 116

figs
   Green bean salad with grilled haloumi &
      rum-soaked figs 73
Filo cigars with nettles & hummus 60
flatbread
   Quick flatbreads 108
   Warm flatbreads 245
Fool's pasta with baby spinach 40
freekeh
   Shaved brussels sprouts & freekeh salad 162
Fresh artichoke salad with lemon, celery & herbs 14
frittata
   Jerusalem artichoke & potato frittata 213
fritters
   Black bean & jalapeño fritters with avocado &
      corn salsa 68
   Zucchini, mint & cheese fritters 116

G
galette
   Asparagus & fennel galette with goat's cheese 26
garlic
   Garlic olive crumbs 18
   Fennel soup 23
   Garlic confit with warm flatbreads 245
   Garlic vinegar dressing 22
   Lime & garlic dressing 31
   Roasted garlic soup with parmesan paprika
      croutons 241
   Sesame cashews 34
   Smoky polenta with garlic & silverbeet 54
gazpacho
   Asian gazpacho 96
ginger
   Ginger-spiced pistachios 134
   Lime, ginger & peanut dipping sauce 217
   Miso ginger baby squash with sesame
      cucumber salad 130
   Roast sweet potato with miso & ginger
      caramel 212
gnocchi
   Sweet potato gnocchi with sage burnt
      butter 204
goat's cheese
   Asparagus & fennel galette with goat's
      cheese 26
   Jalapeños stuffed with roasted-garlic goat's
      cheese 100
   Roast turnips with goat's cheese &
      dukkah 190
grapefruit
   Shaved fennel salad with citrus 28
grapes
   Shaved fennel salad with citrus 28
gratin
   Carrot, cauliflower, broccoli & mustard
      gratin 174
   Fennel gratin 21
green beans see beans, green

green curry
   Spinach & green curry coconut soup 39
green papaya
   Banana blossom & green papaya salad 31
   Jicama & green papaya rice paper rolls 217
greens
   Green sauce 206
   Ultra-greens soup 41
Grilled leeks with agrodolce 236
Grilled witlof with cranberry & pistachio 56

H
haloumi
   Green bean salad with grilled haloumi &
      rum-soaked figs 73
Hasselback potatoes with butter & sage 196
herbs
   Fresh artichoke salad with lemon, celery &
      herbs 14
   Herbed ricotta 143
   see also basil; coriander; dill; mint; parsley,
      rocket; sage
hollandaise sauce
   Miso hollandaise 147
honey
   Black vinegar dipping sauce 227
   Honey-spiced macadamias 137
hummus
   Filo cigars with nettles & hummus 60

I
Indian pumpkin pickle 133
Indian-style tomato chutney 97

J
jalapeño
   Black bean & jalapeño fritters with avocado &
      corn salsa 68
   Green sauce 206
   Jalapeños stuffed with roasted-garlic goat's
      cheese 100
   Potato, cheddar & jalapeño croquettes 202
   Spicy avocado & watermelon salad with mint &
      jalapeño chilli 113
Jerusalem artichoke
   Dill fettuccine with Jerusalem artichoke 216
   Jerusalem artichoke & potato frittata 213
   Jerusalem artichoke soup with chunky
      sourdough croutons & hazelnuts 214
jicama
   Jicama & green papaya rice paper rolls 217
   Jicama & mango salad 218
   Jicama & mango tostadas 218

K
Kaffir coconut dressing 177
kale
   Kale, ricotta & feta rolls 154

Mushroom pot pie with a creamy kohlrabi &
   kale mash 228
Orzo salad with kale, broccoli & lemon 144
Roasted broccolini, kale & chickpeas with
   herbed ricotta 143
Ultra-greens soup 41
kimchi
   health benefits 156
   Kimchi with turmeric 156
   storing 157
kohlrabi
   Mushroom pot pie with a creamy kohlrabi &
      kale mash 228
   Raw kohlrabi & cabbage salad with peanut, lime
      & sesame dressing 164

L
leeks
   Grilled leeks with agrodolce 236
   Leek & potato soup 238
lemon
   Celeriac & lemon mash with mustard &
      buttermilk 182
   Fresh artichoke salad with lemon, celery &
      herbs 14
   Lemon vinaigrette 14
   Lemon yoghurt dressing 14
   Mushroom & ricotta ravioli with a lemon cream
      sauce 224
   Orzo salad with kale, broccoli & lemon 144
   Ricotta-stuffed zucchini flowers 12
   Salsa verde 42
   Squash with lemon & basil 120
   Steamed beans with lemon & pistachio
      dukkah 67
lentils
   Braised silverbeet & lentils 48
   Mexican zucchini, peas & corn salad 122
   Moroccan pumpkin, sweet potato & lentil
      soup 132
   Whole baked sweet potatoes with lentils, feta
      & olives 211
lettuce
   Braised lettuce with broad beans & peas 45
   Charred baby cos with salsa verde 42
lime juice
   Green sauce 206
   Lime & cayenne dressing 122
   Lime & chilli dressing 126
   Lime, chilli & shoyu dressing 217
   Lime & garlic dressing 31
   Lime, ginger & peanut dipping sauce 217
   Lime & sesame dressing 119
   Peanut, lime & sesame dressing 164
   Roasted eggplant with chipotle & lime 103
lotus
   Lotus root chips 178
   Lotus root, water chestnut & edamame
      stir-fry 181

M

mango
    Jicama & mango salad 218
    Jicama & mango tostadas 218
    Radish & mango salad 193
    Zucchini, mango & green bean salad 126
maple syrup
    Roasted maple sprouts with pecans 167
mayonnaise
    Aquafaba mayo 184
    Chipotle mayo 81
    Sriracha mayo 128
    Togarashi mayo 84
Mexican zucchini, peas & corn salad 122
mint
    Cauliflower 'steaks' with tahini & mint dressing 152
    Coriander & mint pesto 172
    Fresh artichoke salad with lemon, celery & herbs 14
    Sautéed zucchini with mint & pine nuts 123
    Smashed edamame with mint & soba noodles 74
    Spicy avocado & watermelon salad with mint & jalapeño chilli 113
    Tahini & mint dressing 152
    Zucchini, mint & cheese fritters 116
miso
    Miso eggplant & soba noodle salad 106
    Miso ginger baby squash with sesame cucumber salad 130
    Miso hollandaise 147
    Roast sweet potato with miso & ginger caramel 212
Mixed Asian mushroom stir-fry on a crisp noodle nest 223
Mixed vegetable pickle 158
Moroccan pumpkin, sweet potato & lentil soup 132
mung beans, split dried
    Spicy pumpkin dhal 138
mushrooms
    Mixed Asian mushroom stir-fry on a crisp noodle nest 223
    Mushroom & chestnut soup with truffled chestnuts & crème fraîche 230
    Mushroom pot pie with a creamy kohlrabi & kale mash 228
    Mushroom & ricotta ravioli with a lemon cream sauce 224
    Mushroom, tomato & barley 'risotto' 231
    Mushroom & water chestnut pot stickers 226
    Stir-fried watercress & baby tatsoi with baby king mushrooms 59
mustard
    Carrot, cauliflower, broccoli & mustard gratin 174
    Celeriac, brown onion & mustard tart 187
    Celeriac & lemon mash with mustard & buttermilk 182
    Orange mustard dressing 46

N

nashi pears
    Pan-tossed turnips & nashi with stilton 188
nettles
    Filo cigars with nettles & hummus 60
noodles *see* egg noodles; soba noodles
nuts
    Grilled witlof with cranberry & pistachio 56
    Honey-spiced macadamias 137
    Jerusalem artichoke soup with chunky sourdough croutons & hazelnuts 214
    Lime, ginger & peanut dipping sauce 217
    Raw kohlrabi & cabbage salad with peanut, lime & sesame dressing 164
    Roasted maple sprouts with pecans 167
    Roasted parsnips with hazelnuts & feta 171
    Wax beans with candied walnuts & feta 70
    see also cashews; peanuts; pecans; pistachios; walnuts

O

Okonomiyaki 161
okra
    Pickled okra 87
olives
    Garlic olive crumbs 18
    Whole baked sweet potatoes with lentils, feta & olives 211
onions
    Ann's potato, cheese & onion pie 200
    Cashew & onion pilau 234
    Celeriac, brown onion & mustard tart 187
    Onion bhajis 242
    Onion soup with stilton toasts 235
    Onion tarte tatin 233
orange
    Orange mustard dressing 46
    Orange & pomegranate dressing 162
    Shaved fennel salad with citrus 28
Orzo salad with kale, broccoli & lemon 144

P

Pan-tossed turnips & nashi with stilton 188
Panzanella 92
papaya *see* green papaya
paprika
    Roasted garlic soup with parmesan paprika croutons 241
Parmesan paprika croutons 241
parsley
    Fresh artichoke salad with lemon, celery & herbs 14
parsnips
    Roasted parsnips with hazelnuts & feta 171
pasta
    Artichoke, basil & baby pea lasagne 24
    Dill fettuccine with Jerusalem artichoke 216
    Fool's pasta with baby spinach 40
    Mushroom & ricotta ravioli with a lemon cream sauce 224
peanuts
    Lime, ginger & peanut dipping sauce 217
    Peanut, lime & sesame dressing 164
peas
    Artichoke, basil & baby pea lasagne 24
    Braised broad beans with artichoke, peas & dill 79
    Braised lettuce with broad beans & peas 45
    Pea & cannellini bean mash with basil oil 77
pea shoots
    Salad of pea shoots & watercress with soy eggs 32
pecans
    Roasted maple sprouts with pecans 167
pesto
    Coriander & mint pesto 172
pickles
    Daikon pickle 191
    Indian pumpkin pickle 133
    Mixed vegetable pickle 158
    Pickled okra 87
    Pickled rainbow chard stems 57
    Pickled shallots 240
Pickling vinegar 158
pie
    Ann's potato, cheese & onion pie 200
pilau
    Cashew & onion pilau 234
pine nuts
    Sautéed zucchini with mint & pine nuts 123
pistachios
    Ginger-spiced pistachios 134
    Grilled witlof with cranberry & pistachio 56
    Pistachio dukkah 67
polenta
    Smoky polenta with garlic & silverbeet 54
pomegranate
    Orange & pomegranate dressing 162
    Roast cauliflower with pomegranate & yoghurt 148
potatoes
    Ann's potato, cheese & onion pie 200
    Crispy potato stacks 199
    Hasselback potatoes with butter & sage 196
    Jerusalem artichoke & potato frittata 213
    Leek & potato soup 238
    Potato, cheddar & jalapeño croquettes 202
    Red pepper rouille on kipflers with toasted walnuts 98
    Super-crunchy roasted potatoes 198
    Sweet potato gnocchi with sage burnt butter 204

pumpkin
Biryani-stuffed pumpkins 134
Indian pumpkin pickle 133
Moroccan pumpkin, sweet potato & lentil soup 132
Pumpkin crisps with honey-spiced macadamias 137
Red curry pumpkin dip 139
Spicy pumpkin dhal 138

Q
Quick flatbreads 108

R
radishes
Radish & mango salad 193
Salad of pea shoots & watercress with soy eggs 32
rainbow chard
Pickled rainbow chard stems 57
Rainbow slaw with avocado dressing 102
raisins
Cabbage rolls stuffed with black rice & raisins 165
Raita 82
Raw beetroot relish with sesame 185
Raw kohlrabi & cabbage salad with peanut, lime & sesame dressing 164
Red curry pumpkin dip 139
Red wine vinegar dressing 28
relish
Raw beetroot relish with sesame 185
remoulade
Celeriac & rocket remoulade with aquafaba mayo 184
rhubarb
Spiced rhubarb chutney 35
rice
Cashew & onion pilau 234
Spanakopita 51
see also black rice
rice paper rolls
Jicama & green papaya rice paper rolls 217
ricotta
Artichoke, basil & baby pea lasagne 24
Asparagus & fennel galette with goat's cheese 26
Filo cigars with nettles & hummus 60
Herbed ricotta 143
Kale, ricotta & feta rolls 154
Mushroom & ricotta ravioli with a lemon cream sauce 224
Ricotta-stuffed zucchini flowers 12
Roasted broccolini, kale & chickpeas with herbed ricotta 143
Spanakopita 51
Zucchini, mint & cheese fritters 116
Roast cauliflower with pomegranate & yoghurt 148

Roast sweet potato with miso & ginger caramel 212
Roast turnips with goat's cheese & dukkah 190
Roasted broccolini, kale & chickpeas with herbed ricotta 143
Roasted carrot soup with coriander & mint pesto 172
Roasted eggplant with chipotle & lime 103
Roasted garlic soup with parmesan paprika croutons 241
Roasted maple sprouts with pecans 167
Roasted parsnips with hazelnuts & feta 171
rocket
Celeriac & rocket remoulade with aquafaba mayo 184
rouille
Red pepper rouille on kipflers with toasted walnuts 98

S
sage
Hasselback potatoes with butter & sage 196
Sweet potato gnocchi with sage burnt butter 204
salads
Baba ghanoush & tomato salad with quick flatbreads 108
Banana blossom & green papaya salad 31
Cauliflower 'tabbouleh' salad 150
Fresh artichoke salad with lemon, celery & herbs 14
Green bean & burghul salad with currants & crisp-fried capers 66
Green bean salad with grilled haloumi & rum-soaked figs 73
Jicama & mango salad 218
Mexican zucchini, peas & corn salad 122
Miso eggplant & soba noodle salad 106
Miso ginger baby squash with sesame cucumber salad 130
Orzo salad with kale, broccoli & lemon 144
Radish & mango salad 193
Raw kohlrabi & cabbage salad with peanut, lime & sesame dressing 164
Salad of pea shoots & watercress with soy eggs 32
Shaved brussels sprouts & freekeh salad 162
Shaved fennel salad with citrus 28
Snow pea & sesame salad 78
Spiced roasted baby carrot salad with kaffir coconut dressing 177
Spicy avocado & watermelon salad with mint & jalapeño chilli 113
Sumac chickpea salad with fennel & artichoke 22
Watercress salad with burrata 46
Zucchini, mango & green bean salad 126
Zucchini 'noodle' salad with lime & sesame dressing 119
see also slaw

salsa
Avocado & corn salsa 68
Salsa verde 42
Tomatillo salsa 95
Salt-cured egg yolks 17
sauces
Green sauce 206
Miso hollandaise 147
Salsa verde 42
Tamarind sauce 82
see also dipping sauce
Sautéed zucchini with mint & pine nuts 123
schnitzels
Eggplant schnitzels with buttermilk slaw 104
sesame
Black sesame dressing 52
Lime & sesame dressing 119
Peanut, lime & sesame dressing 164
Raw beetroot relish with sesame 185
Sesame cashews 34
Sesame cucumber salad 130
Snow pea & sesame salad 78
Steamed choy sum with sesame cashews 34
Zucchini 'noodle' salad with lime & sesame dressing 119
shallots
Onion tarte tatin 233
Pickled shallots 240
Shaved brussels sprouts & freekeh salad 162
Shaved fennel salad with citrus 28
shoyu
Lime, chilli & shoyu dressing 217
Sichuan eggplant 107
silverbeet
Braised silverbeet & lentils 48
Smoky polenta with garlic & silverbeet 54
Ultra-greens soup 41
slaw
Eggplant schnitzels with buttermilk slaw 104
Rainbow slaw with avocado dressing 102
Smashed edamame with mint & soba noodles 74
Smoky polenta with garlic & silverbeet 54
Snake bean, vegetable & tofu curry 64
Snow pea & sesame salad 78
soba noodles
Amaranth with soba noodles & black sesame dressing 52
Miso eggplant & soba noodle salad 106
Smashed edamame with mint & soba noodles 74
soup
Asian gazpacho 96
Fennel soup 23
Fool's pasta with baby spinach 40
Jerusalem artichoke soup with chunky sourdough croutons & hazelnuts 214
Leek & potato soup 238
Moroccan pumpkin, sweet potato & lentil soup 132

Mushroom & chestnut soup with truffled chestnuts & crème fraîche 230
Onion soup with stilton toasts 235
Roasted carrot soup with coriander & mint pesto 172
Roasted garlic soup with parmesan paprika croutons 241
Spinach & green curry coconut soup 39
Three-way cauliflower soup 151
Ultra-greens soup 41
Sourdough croutons 215
soy sauce
    Black vinegar dipping sauce 226
    Peanut, lime & sesame dressing 164
    Soy eggs 32
Spaghetti squash patties with sriracha mayo 128
Spanakopita 51
Spanakorizo 49
Spiced roasted baby carrot salad with kaffir coconut dressing 177
Spicy avocado & watermelon salad with mint & jalapeño chilli 113
Spicy pumpkin dhal 138
spinach
    Fool's pasta with baby spinach 40
    Spanakopita 51
    Spanakorizo 49
    Spinach & green curry coconut soup 39
spring onions
    Artichoke, basil & baby pea lasagne 24
    Green sauce 206
squash
    Miso ginger baby squash with sesame cucumber salad 130
    Spaghetti squash patties with sriracha mayo 128
    Squash with lemon & basil 120
Sriracha mayo 128
Steamed beans with lemon & pistachio dukkah 67
Steamed choy sum with sesame cashews 34
stilton
    Onion soup with stilton toasts 235
    Pan-tossed turnips & nashi with stilton 188
stir-fry
    Bean sprouts stir-fry in egg net 86
    Lotus root, water chestnut & edamame stir-fry 181
    Mixed Asian mushroom stir-fry on a crisp noodle nest 223
    Stir-fried watercress & baby tatsoi with baby king mushrooms 59
stock
    Vegetable stock 23
Stuffed tomatoes 90
Sumac chickpea salad with fennel & artichoke 22
Super-crunchy roasted potatoes 198
Sweet & sour cucumber 110
sweet potato
    Moroccan pumpkin, sweet potato & lentil soup 132

Roast sweet potato with miso & ginger caramel 212
Sweet potato & celeriac bake 208
Sweet potato & corn empanadas 206
Sweet potato gnocchi with sage burnt butter 204
Whole baked sweet potatoes with lentils, feta & olives 211

T
'tabbouleh' 150
    Cauliflower 'tabbouleh' salad 150
Tahini & mint dressing 152
Tamarind sauce 82
tarragon
    Shaved fennel salad with citrus 28
tart
    Celeriac, brown onion & mustard tart 187
    Onion tarte tatin 233
tatsoi
    Stir-fried watercress & baby tatsoi with baby king mushrooms 59
Temper topping 138
Tempura baby corn with togarashi mayo 84
Three-way cauliflower soup 151
tikkis
    Corn tikkis with raita & tamarind sauce 83
tofu
    Snake bean, vegetable & tofu curry 64
Togarashi mayo 84
tomatillo
    Charred tomatillo tostadas 95
tomatoes
    Asian gazpacho 96
    Baba ghanoush & tomato salad with quick flatbreads 108
    Cauliflower 'tabbouleh' salad 150
    Indian-style tomato chutney 97
    Mushroom, tomato & barley 'risotto' 231
    Panzanella 92
    Stuffed tomatoes 90
tostadas
    Charred tomatillo tostadas 95
    Jicama & mango tostadas 218
truffles
    Fennel soup 23
    Mushroom & chestnut soup with truffled chestnuts & crème fraîche 230
    Truffle aioli 125
turmeric
    Kimchi with turmeric 156
turnips
    Pan-tossed turnips & nashi with stilton 188
    Roast turnips with goat's cheese & dukkah 190

U
Ultra-greens soup 41

V
vegetables
    Mixed vegetable pickle 158
    Snake bean, vegetable & tofu curry 64
    Vegetable stock 23
    see also specific vegetables
vinegar
    Black vinegar dipping sauce 226
    Garlic vinegar dressing 22
    pickling vinegar 158
    Red wine vinegar dressing 28

W
walnuts
    Red pepper rouille on kipflers with toasted walnuts 98
    Wax beans with candied walnuts & feta 70
Warm flatbreads 245
water chestnut
    Lotus root, water chestnut & edamame stir-fry 181
    Mushroom & water chestnut pot stickers 226
watercress
    Salad of pea shoots & watercress with soy eggs 32
    Stir-fried watercress & baby tatsoi with baby king mushrooms 59
    Watercress salad with burrata 46
watermelon
    Spicy avocado & watermelon salad with mint & jalapeño chilli 113
Wax beans with candied walnuts & feta 70
wheat grains
    Fresh artichoke salad with lemon, celery & herbs 14
Whole baked sweet potatoes with lentils, feta & olives 211
wholemeal flour 26
witlof
    Grilled witlof with cranberry & pistachio 56

Y
yoghurt
    Lemon yoghurt dressing 14
    Roast cauliflower with pomegranate & yoghurt 148

Z
zucchini
    Crumbed zucchini batons with truffle aioli 125
    Mexican zucchini, peas & corn salad 122
    Sautéed zucchini with mint & pine nuts 123
    Zucchini, mango & green bean salad 126
    Zucchini, mint & cheese fritters 116
    Zucchini 'noodle' salad with lime & sesame dressing 119
zucchini flowers
    Ricotta-stuffed zucchini flowers 12

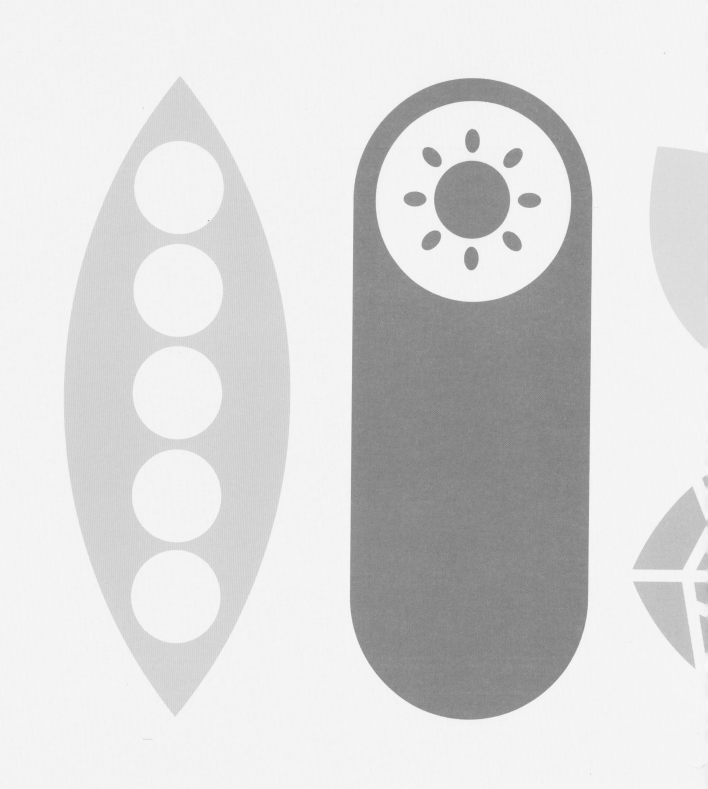